C. NORTHCOTE PARKINSON'S

PARKINSON'S
LAW

C. NORTHCOTE PARKINSON'S

PARKINSON'S LAW

A MODERN-DAY INTERPRETATION
OF A MANAGEMENT CLASSIC
BY LEO GOUGH

infiniteideas

First published in 2011 by
Infinite Ideas Limited
36 St Giles
Oxford
OX1 3LD
United Kingdom
www.infideas.com

A CIP catalogue record for this book is available from the British Library

ISBN 978–1–906821–34–0

Designed by Darren Hayball
Typeset by Sparks – www.sparkspublishing.com
Printed and bound in Great Britain

BRILLIANT IDEAS

INTRODUCTION

Nobody really wants more bureaucracy and red tape. Governments and multinational companies spend vast sums on trying to make their bureaucracies more efficient. Some management consultants spend their entire careers trying to cure dysfunctional administrative systems. Stock market analysts preach the need for 'lean organisations'. Consumers complain of faceless corporations and government departments that can't seem to perform simple tasks in a timely fashion.

So, if nobody wants more bureaucracy, why does it just keep on growing? The answer is Parkinson's Law. According to Parkinson's Law, bureaucracies tend to expand for two main reasons: first, that bureaucrats naturally make extra work for each other, and second, that bureaucrats like to increase the number of people they are in charge of. What's more, the growth in personnel bears no relation to the productivity of the organisation. The Law proposes that 'Work expands to fill the time available for its completion'. In other words, in the average administrative office, everyone will always be busy, no matter how much, or how little, real work has to be done.

Cyril Northcote Parkinson was an obscure professor of history at a university in Singapore when he wrote *Parkinson's Law* in the late 1950s. Based on an essay he published in *The Economist* magazine, it appeared as a book in 1958 and became an instant bestseller worldwide. It's a gem of a book, stylish, witty, and satirical, that cuts through all the management theory guff to show how and why bureaucracies waste time. Parkinson became a celebrity and, after a few years as visiting professor at Harvard and Berkeley, gave up teaching to become a full-time writer and lecturer.

Because it was written in the 1950s, Parkinson's book reflects the norms of the time; for example, managers and bureaucrats are generally assumed to male, and the secretaries are assumed to be female. Some of the references to racial and cultural bias may make the modern reader feel a little queasy. Nevertheless, Parkinson was ahead of his time. He would have laughed at the explosion in management theory and business schools, and at the worldwide efforts of governments to make their civil services run more like businesses – all exercises in futility, he would have said. *Parkinson's Law – A Modern-Day Interpretation of a Management Classic* shows how you can apply his devastating critique of office life to analyse, and perhaps resolve, the frustrations we all experience, whether we are consumers, committee members, managers, office workers or civil servants.

1 'MAKE-WORK' IN ACTION

Politicians and taxpayers have assumed (with occasional phases of doubt) that a rising total in the number of civil servants must reflect a growing volume of work to be done … The fact is that the number of the officials and the quantity of the work are not related to each other at all.

Parkinson wrote his book at the height of the era of state-directed economies, when the public sector was far larger than it is today. Since the 1980s, most governments around the world have tried very hard to reduce the size of their countries' public sectors – especially through the drive for privatisation – and to make their employees more efficient and accountable. Similarly, multinationals have gone to enormous lengths to cut the dead weight out of their organisations. The trouble is, bureaucracy has a strange way of creeping back, like a fungus.

Why is this? Parkinson points to the essential problem: in any kind of office, it is easy to create unnecessary tasks with the best of intentions. Often, it is extremely difficult to judge whether a given administrative chore is worth doing – they always *seem* worthwhile, especially to workers who have no overall picture of the process. Unless there are eagle-eyed managers who are obsessed with overall efficiency, office tasks will just naturally grow and grow, and more and more people will be needed to push the paper around.

Not long ago I was invited by a foreign government to go on an all-expenses-paid inspection tour of various locations in their country. No date for the trip was given. I applied in November and forgot all about it. Nearly eight months later, in June, I was asked for my passport details, address and other personal details. The next month, I was asked for my personal email address. The process went on and on. I had contact with seven different officials in three different cities. I had to give the same information to them again and again. They changed the date of the trip three times. I received and sent a total of 112 emails, and had 27 telephone conversations. I finally went on the trip two years after my original application. We didn't go anywhere that needed any special security clearance. I could have easily made the same trip as an ordinary tourist, and it would have cost me only £1500. I could have organised it in two days.

The country wasn't a failed state, or a 'less developed country'; most official publications list it as a modernising, westernised, success story. So what went wrong? Every civil servant is afraid of upsetting their boss. Senior officials issue arbitrary orders and everyone scrambles to obey. Nobody ever tries to match time expended to results achieved. The result? Gross, stupendous incompetence that would put any commercial organisation out of business.

HERE'S AN IDEA FOR YOU

Never lose your temper with a bureaucrat. Be co-operative, patient and polite, and never give up. Seven times out of ten you'll eventually get what you want because your file will have grown so big that they'll eventually become desperate to close it once and for all.

2 FULL EMPLOYMENT

Those who hold that growth is essential to give full employment are fully entitled to their opinion.

This argument has been much used by the European social democracies: having people paid to do nothing useful is better than having lean, efficient, productive organisations and less than full employment. This view does have some validity. During the Depression of the 1930s, for example, people with money became reluctant to invest in companies and preferred to put their money into government bonds. Industry became unable to borrow and went into crisis, creating apalling mass unemployment. The great economist J.M. Keynes argued at the time that it would be better for the government to pay people to dig holes and then fill them up than to leave them without work. He was right, in the 1930s, because the world's economy had become gridlocked and governments had to create jobs, however inefficient, as part of a raft of measures to get things moving again.

It does not follow, though, that in other circumstances full employment is necessary or even desirable. If companies are in a position to grow and

DEFINING IDEA

If the Treasury were to fill old bottles with banknotes, bury them at suitable depths in disused coal mines which are then filled up to the surface with town rubbish, and leave it to private enterprise on well tried principals of laissez-faire to dig the notes up again ... there need be no more unemployment.

J.M. KEYNES. ECONOMIST

prosper, forcing them to carry a lot of deadweight employees actually hinders a society's ability to create more wealth. Critics of the centrally planned Soviet system, for example, argue that its artificial creation of near-full employment contributed to its inflexibility, inefficiency and ultimate failure. Most economists these days believe that there should be some unemployment within an economy to allow for things like further study, job-changing and so on – and estimates of the 'optimal' unemployment rates vary from 3–7%. It really becomes a philosophical question: should the government artificially create or subsidise jobs that have no really useful purpose, just to make sure that wealth is distributed to everyone, or are there other, better ways of providing incentives for people to work and for organisations to provide work that will make the whole nation richer?

Parkinson was clearly against allowing bureaucracies to grow just to create jobs, because he deplored the increase in inefficiency. And his great contribution was to point out that you don't need the interference of a well-meaning government for this to happen: bureaucracies just naturally do this by themselves!

HERE'S AN IDEA FOR YOU

Research suggests that the vast majority of jobs are not advertised – most are filled internally or by employee recommendation. So how do you get to hear about them? Use social networking! And don't go around asking people about jobs when you are networking; look for information about the people and organisations you are targeting. Find out what their needs and preoccupations are. That way, you will know exactly how to present yourself when opportunities arise. Typically, the best opportunities are one-off projects where the employer is under pressure to solve a problem; if you can solve it, you're hired! Once you are hired, you can work on ways of turning the one-off project into a permanent position.

3 COMMITTEES

[As committees grew] relatively few [members] were chosen from any idea that they are or could be or ever have been useful. A majority were brought in merely to conciliate some outside group.

Parkinson really had it in for committees, and was one of the great promoters of the idea that they are generally pretty useless. But it is difficult to see how else you could organise a group decision-making process in many situations. What is noticeable, though, is that groups that are put together to plan a project within a hierarchical organisation, like a company, seem to be more effective than ones that are a collection of people representing conflicting interests and where there is no chain of command. It is these latter bodies, often organised by a highly bureaucratic institution in order to 'gain consensus' by appeasing a range of interest groups, that Parkinson is criticising here.

DEFINING IDEA

Muddle is the extra unknown personality in any committee
ANTHONY SAMPSON,
MANAGEMENT WRITER

Perhaps the classic example of an ineffective committee is the international Non-Intervention Committee, established to prevent other countries from sending military aid to the belligerents in the Spanish Civil War. Civil war had broken out in Spain almost by accident in 1936. A right-wing general, Francisco Franco, managed to persuade Hitler and Mussolini to send aircraft to transport his army from North Africa to Spain, and later to provide military equipment and (in the case of Italy)

100,000 extra troops to fight the war. Russia, fearful of fascist expansionism, started sending guns, planes and tanks by sea to the other side, and Britain and France, worrying that the situation would escalate into a war that would engulf the whole of Europe, persuaded all the other European nations to join the Non-Intervention Committee.

The committee proceedings make depressing reading. Plan after plan was produced, first to prevent foreign combatants from entering Spain and then, when those plans had failed, to get the foreign combatants to leave Spain. Russia and the Axis powers lied about their involvement in the war, and the other countries had to smile politely. Across Europe, the public was outraged at what seemed to be the total ineffectiveness of the committee; it looked as if France and Britain were abandoning Spain to the fascists, who were winning the war.

Yet, on another interpretation, the committee was a triumph of bureaucratic cunning. France and Britain were desperately trying to prevent or at least delay the outbreak of what became World War II, which the Spanish Civil War could easily have precipitated in 1936/37. By bringing all the European powers into the committee and burying the discussions in bureaucracy, it was possible to contain the civil war within Spain and prevent it from escalating into a Europe-wide war. It was hard luck on the Spanish republic, of course, but some historians argue that it bought vital time for the Allies to prepare to fight World War II when it finally broke out in 1939.

HERE'S AN IDEA FOR YOU

If you really want to make quick decisions, keep committees small. Larger committees may be necessary in order to achieve compromises with rival forces, but they have more devious uses; as was the case with the Non-Intervention Committee, they can be used to buy time to improve your own position.

4 ENTREPRENEURIAL VALUES

In the American log cabin story the point is soon reached at which the future millionaire must wear a tie.

C.N. Parkinson was unusual in that he spent a long time as a university lecturer in the Far East, mainly in Singapore, at a time (the 1950s) when it was only just beginning to recover from the ravages of World War II. When his book first came out, therefore, his chapter on the Chinese entrepreneurs of southeast Asia (Chapter 7, 'From Palm Thatch to Packard') must have seemed very eccentric indeed. In those days the Far East represented no economic threat whatsoever to the West and looked set to remain a very undeveloped region of the world that suffered from dire poverty and disease in many areas.

DEFINING IDEA

Nobody talks of entrepreneurship as survival, but that's exactly what it is and what nurtures creative thinking.

ANITA RODDICK, FOUNDER OF THE BODY SHOP

Today, however, Japan, the Asian Tiger countries and latterly China and India, have become powerful economies. Parkinson's comments now seem amazingly prescient as Far Eastern businesspeople are demonstrating great aptitude and creativity in all kinds of industries, and have become increasingly able to challenge Western products and services on their own terms. In his 'log cabin' comment Parkinson is praising the traditional frugality of Chinese businesspeople; especially in the early period of amassing a fortune, there is often much less social pressure to flaunt your prosperity than there is in the West. Of course, in modern cities like Singapore and Hong Kong many people are, if anything, even more obsessed with conspicuous consumption than they are in the West, but there is still a greater awareness in the East of the possibility and consequences of failure.

That's one of the main reasons for being thrifty even in times of plenty: to channel your resources into productive activities and to keep the discipline of living within your means. Very few successful entrepreneurs have a smooth, easy ride to the top. Most often, they go through some periods of extreme hardship and stress, when they have to display an impressive array of survival skills. And being a shopaholic – or indeed, any other kind of -holic – has no part in being a true survivor.

Suppose, for example, you have an opportunity to go on a foreign business trip that will cost your entire travel budget for the next five years, but has the potential to generate some big contracts. Should you be thrifty and turn it down? Or should you take the risk of spending the money and failing to land any new business? There is no easy answer – it all depends on the circumstances, and on your own capacity to make a realistic assessment of the risk/reward ratio. One thing is for sure, though: if your real reason for going on the trip is just to have a holiday, you're probably wasting your time.

HERE'S AN IDEA FOR YOU

Should you be thrifty? Most small business people would immediately say 'Yes', but don't confuse thrift with a rigid outlook – in both the public and the private sectors, the really successful leaders have to take some risks. When faced with a proposal to make some 'extraordinary' expenditure, don't just consider the risk, consider the ratio of risk to reward; if you take no risks at all, your organisation will surely stagnate.

5 USELESS ACTIVITY

No one has been idle. All have done their best.

DEFINING IDEA

The brain is a wonderful organ. It starts working the moment you get up in the morning, and does not stop until you get into the office.
ROBERT FROST

Perhaps it is easier to see how public sector bureaucracies are liable to lose sight of their real objectives than it is to see that large commercial organisations often do the same thing. You might think that all those big corporations that are quoted on the stock market and have annual sales figures that are bigger than some countries' GDPs are run with a slick, clinical efficiency, ever mindful of their overarching mission: to make more and more profits. Well, some of them are, sometimes. Most of the time, though, the right hand doesn't know what the left hand is doing, and most employees – and even senior managers – forget to ask themselves the question, 'is this activity contributing to the profitability of the firm?'

For example, when planning the marketing of a new product, it is quite common to assume that by increasing sales, or capturing a larger share of a market, greater profits will naturally follow. Nothing could be further from the truth! There is always plenty of over-optimistic and misleading data about markets, and it is easy to make very bad decisions by extrapolating from emerging, but as yet unproven, trends. Millions of pounds and thousands of man-hours can easily be wasted on trying to increase sales with the net result of actually reducing the profits.

Often, unprofitable activities start out by being profitable, but then slowly decay. Take the food industry; during the last two decades there has been a big shift in power from the major food manufacturers, often producing household name brands of foods, to the major supermarket chains. By employing a range of sophisticated techniques, the supermarkets have managed to weaken the strength – and profits – of the manufacturers without reducing the overall supply of food. For example, many supermarkets sell 'own brand' versions of famous products at a slightly lower price than the name brands, and have cut manufacturers' margins to the bone by playing competitors off against each other. Food manufacturers have had to be alert and adaptable to prosper in the changed environment. For example, Coca-Cola and Pepsi now have to rely heavily on the profits of sales of their drinks at restaurants and cafes, rather than from sales of cans and bottles.

Hard work that isn't profitable is worse than useless. You have to spend some time monitoring the value of your activities, or they are liable to lose value as the situation changes. To do that, you have to be able to attach a real monetary value to activities – you need, for example, to know the value of each segment of your market, and what it costs you to reach them.

HERE'S AN IDEA FOR YOU

This may sound a little ruthless, but it's worth doing a similar analysis on your own work patterns – we often spend a lot of time each week doing things that don't really get us anywhere. Try to set clear objectives that are both attainable and worthwhile, and then ask yourself how each of your regular activities has helped you towards these goals.

6 BUREAUCRATIC GROWTH

No attempt has been made to inquire whether departments ought to grow in size.

DEFINING IDEA

I think myself that we have more machinery of government than is necessary, too many parasites living on the labor of the industrious.
THOMAS JEFFERSON

It doesn't seem to matter what ideology or political complexion a government has, or what the aims of its organisations are – government departments just seem to grow and grow.

Take the US: originally, the national bureaucracy was very small (only 50 government employees in 1789), but expanded by 800% during the first half of the 19th century, and gathered even more momentum after the civil war to reach nearly three million employees by the year 2000. Part of this growth can be explained by the growth of the country's population, and of the increased complexity of modern society, but not all of it. For example, in the Department of Agriculture the number of top jobs grew from 80 to 242 between 1960 and 1990, even though farming declined in terms of land size, number of farm workers and the number of farms during that period. What's more, unlike commercial organisations, government departments rarely get closed down; according to one study, between 1923 and 1973, 85% of federal departments survived and 246 new ones were created.

In the European Community, the figures make even more depressing reading. Although the European Commission goes out of its way to claim that the number of employees in EU institutions is very low, independent studies suggest that the number has now reached 170,000 – substantially larger than the size of the British army – having grown by between 10 and 20% during the last decade, depending on which study you believe. The main activity of these administrators is to prepare pan-European legislation, and the number of new laws and regulations they produce is growing too. In 1998 the UK adopted 595 EC regulations; in 2008 it adopted more than 2000.

The situation in the developing world is no better. During the last two decades the Arab countries, for instance, have enjoyed a doubling – and in some cases a trebling – of the number of government departments and agencies.

Perhaps the most striking example of bureaucratic growth is that of the international Non-Governmental Organisations, or NGOs. Despite their name, NGOs are actually quite close to governments, receiving most of their funding from them and increasingly gaining access to policy-makers through organisations like the World Bank, WTO and the World Economic Forum. There were about 5000 NGOS in 1975; now there are more than 50,000, spending nearly $2 trillion a year, which makes the sector larger economically than all but four of world's nations!

HERE'S AN IDEA FOR YOU

You'll never get anywhere with a bureaucracy, public or private, unless you learn all its jargon and technical concepts. For example, people always complain about their banks without ever bothering to learn how their systems really work. Once you have understood how banks operate, you can talk to them without losing your temper and, more often than not, get what you really want. It's the same with government departments; learn about their chain of command, their responsibilities and their processes. When you talk to them they will realise that you are well-informed, and they'll treat you more professionally.

7 THE BUREAUCRATIC INCENTIVES

An official wants to multiply subordinates, not rivals.

So, if bureaucracies have a natural tendency to grow in spite of periodic efforts to reduce them, what is the cause? One answer may be that the incentives for a bureaucrat are quite different from those of an employee in a normal firm. Company employees may be power-hungry, selfish, greedy, lazy, and so on – in other words, have normal human failings – but in most cases they are constrained by the nature of their organisations: companies tend to value profits more highly than unprofitable expansion, so someone who tries to build a little empire within a firm will generally have to justify it by continuously producing increased profits.

DEFINING IDEA

Government runs on the idea that the more things you do, the more effective you are.
PETER DRUCKER

The reverse is true in government bureaucracies. They aren't motivated by profit. They don't go broke, and they tend not to fire their employees. In spite of efforts in recent years to make the way bureaucrats' performance is judged more like the way commercial employees are judged, it is still very difficult to assess the performance of individuals and departments. It is almost impossible to know, for example, how well they have used their resources, or how effective they have been. Bureaucracies are allocated money through a budget and the results are judged ultimately not by the behaviour of customers in a marketplace, but by officials and politicians higher up in the organisational chain.

To gain status and to get noticed as a bureaucrat, you need growth. It is hard, at least in well-run bureaucracies, for bureaucrats to steal money or to get bonuses for good work. You make money by staying in for the long term, by collecting your pension, and by climbing, usually slowly, up a rigid system of pay grades. But if you can gradually poach responsibilities from other departments and get authorisation to have more subordinates working for you, and you can convince your superiors that all this is in some way in the public interest, you'll continue to get promoted.

In the US, where public accountability seems to be taken more seriously than in most other countries, it is occasionally possible to find real evidence of bureaucratic waste. For example, in 2005 the space agency NASA was found to have a large fleet of aircraft that it used to ferry executives to and from meetings. It was a popular service within the organisation and NASA explained that, while its managers could indeed take commercial flights to their meetings, using its own planes saved time at airports and made it easier to do work during flights. All that sounded reasonable, until it was established that each flight cost NASA more than five times the price of a commercial air ticket – in direct contravention of a government directive that such flights should never cost more than a commercial flight.

HERE'S AN IDEA FOR YOU

When dealing with a bureaucrat – and especially when you are trying to get them to change their minds – it is really important to listen to what they have to say. Bureaucrats won't give any ground unless they think that you have listened to them and understood their points. Listening really works – and the more they speak, the more information they will give that will enable you to negotiate.

8 WORK EXPANDS...

Work expands so as to fill the time available for its completion.

As Parkinson pointed out, this phenomenon is not confined to bureaucracies. He gives the example of an elderly lady who takes all day to write a letter, find a stamp and go to the post box. The problem is well-known to people who are unemployed; finding oneself facing a vista of unstructured days, it's easy to take a long time to achieve very little.

The same is true at work, if there aren't clearly defined objectives and the pressure to meet them. Bureaucracies tend to have a lot of rules and structures, but not much motivation to finish jobs quickly. After all, the longer a project takes and the more people involved, the more the organisation grows. Individual employees may work hard and manage their time as efficiently as possible, but as long as the higher-ups see no advantage in getting services running quickly or in making customer satisfaction important, useless work will just grow and grow.

DEFINING IDEA

There is no passion like that of a functionary for his function.

GEORGES CLEMENCEAU,
FRENCH PRIME MINISTER
1917–1920

It used to be the Soviet countries that were the worst culprits but, according to a recent World Bank study called 'Doing Business in 2010', it now seems to be sub-Saharan Africa and Latin America. For example, if you want to start a new business in Hong Kong, you have to go through three legal procedures, while in Brazil and Venezuela there are sixteen.

Venezuela comes out as the worst Latin American country to do business in, according to the study, and now has the strictest employment laws in the world: a boss of a private company is not allowed to fire an employee for any reason. Oil-rich Venezuela has been notorious for its out-of-control bureaucracy for decades. From the late 1960s, the government started creating a large number of new state-owned enterprises at a rate of eight a year, growing to fifty a year by 1975. By the 1990s, an estimated one million people were employed doing useless jobs in the public sector, from the four doormen employed to open a single door and the lift operators in automatic lifts to the (now bankrupt) state airline which employed 24 pilots for each of its planes.

Whatever you think of the country's colourful president, Hugo Chavez, you have to admire his aim of reforming the country's bloated bureaucracy – but a massive programme of nationalisation of most of the country's industries is perhaps not the best way to achieve it. Law and order is breaking down and Caracas is now said to be one of the crime capitals of the world, while the imposition of price controls (always a bureaucratic favourite) has created shortages in basic food staples, like beans, but not in luxuries, like caviar. Bureaucrats are ever more visible. Recently customs officials impounded all non-Venezuelan yachts for two weeks to check that they were not owned by rich Venezuelan tax dodgers – all very commendable, no doubt, but perhaps not the best way to encourage wealthy tourists to come to Venezuela.

HERE'S AN IDEA FOR YOU

Even if you think you know how to manage your time well, you could probably do with a refresher course. Go on one of those gung-ho, take-no-prisoners time management courses – you'll get some great tips.

9 BUREAUCRATIC MALEVOLENCE

Officials make work for each other.

In his book, Parkinson is at pains not to accuse bureaucrats of acting in bad faith. For example, in his axiom that 'officials make work for each other' he stresses the way in which this is done unconsciously, and ignores the cases where it is done deliberately with full knowledge of the consequences. But it is quite clear that bureaucrats often do act deliberately in bad faith. Why? Because it is generally not in their interests to actually achieve the objectives that their organisation has been set; it is much better, from the bureaucrat's point of view, to look as if you are doing your best, and ensure that you are not accountable for the failure to reach the goal.

DEFINING IDEA

Asking a town hall to slim down its staff is like asking an alcoholic to blow up a distillery.

YES MINISTER TV SERIES

For example, back in the days of the USSR, it was common for shops to be virtually empty of goods. When a shipment of, say, soap, came in, people would queue for hours to buy the maximum they were allowed because they didn't know when they would be able to buy it again. The cause was the 'jobsworth' nature of the production and supply system. Everybody just fulfilled their quotas and no more – there was no incentive to be flexible, or to make an extra effort, because you didn't get any reward for your extra effort and indeed you might get into trouble for it.

Although things have improved in the UK during the last 20 years, we still encounter similar examples of 'jobsworth' attitudes, especially in the public sector. Suppose, for instance, there is increased demand at a hospital or a passport office. The bureaucrats spring into action and solve the problem instantly by not allowing any more people into the office. If you are operating a telephone helpline and you get more calls than you anticipated, you can solve the problem by just not answering the phone – and playing canned music to the frustrated callers to make it look like you're doing your best.

Of course, it's not only in the public sector that you find jobsworth officials. A few years back in India I wanted to change some money at a bank in a small town. I had been warned that it might take a few hours. It took seven. I arrived in the morning, as soon as the bank opened, filled in my forms and presented the money to the cashier. Unlike more sophisticated bureaucracies, there was no screen to prevent me from watching what happened next. At first, it looked good. Within five minutes of my handing over the money and the forms, the cashier had taken them to another clerk sitting at a desk behind. There they stayed for an hour or two. During the seven hours I waited, I was interested to watch my papers go from one desk to another (a total of five) until finally they came back to the cashier, and I got my money. Well, the customer's time isn't important, is it?

HERE'S AN IDEA FOR YOU

When dealing with a bureaucracy, always have all your paperwork to hand – and extra copies, spare passport-sized photographs, code words, and all the correspondence filed in date order. At the very least, you'll minimise the delays.

10 HOW SCHEMES GROW WRONG

The thing to be done swells in importance and complexity in a direct ratio with the time to be spent.

It shouldn't, of course, but it often does. Don't think that in these days of open government and better accountability that things have actually improved all that much. In one case in 2008, the House of Commons public accounts committee found that the Department of Transport was guilty of 'stupendous incompetence' in its management of a long-term scheme that was intended to make its bureaucracy more efficient and produce net savings of £57 million. Instead of creating savings, the scheme had wound up costing the taxpayer an extra £81 million, because costs had increased and the planned-for savings were less than expected.

DEFINING IDEA

There are three things that can go wrong with projects: they can cost more; they can take longer; or they can make matters worse.

SIR JOHN BOURN, FORMER UK COMPTROLLER AND AUDITOR GENERAL

The idea had been to create a Shared Services Agency that was going to save time and money as a substitute for all the administrative processes that were being duplicated at the Department of Transport and various allied agencies such as the DVLA. All the agencies were going to develop a standardised way of doing things, and the Shared Services Agency was going to have a wonderful new software system to make it all work.

The software system was provided by IBM and other contractors. Things began to go wrong almost immediately as the Department was unable to get the different agencies to agree on a standardised set of business procedures. The computer system was introduced quickly, without adequate time for testing. People using the computer system found that they had to continue to keep manual records – thus duplicating the work – because the system was always going wrong. One person complained that the system recorded one episode of sick leave because of a broken bone as a 'cold' and another due to bereavement as 'anxiety'. Many people complained that the system often gave messages in German instead of English. Nobody seemed to understand how to use the system, and to get help you had to raise a 'service ticket' and wait for months to get your query answered. There was a helpline, but staff complained that 90% of the information given by the helpdesk was wrong. Many invoices were paid twice while many others were paid late (incurring fines). Some departments stopped sending vital original documents such as marriage certificates internally because they seemed to get lost. The Department was criticised for managing the IT contractors badly, failing to subject them to competitive pressures and allowing costs to skyrocket. As the Chairman for Committee of Public Accounts said to the mandarins at the inquiry, 'This was not a very happy story, was it?'

HERE'S AN IDEA FOR YOU

Doing business with government can be very lucrative, but contracts are hard to get. Long-term planning is essential, as is developing relationships. You have to network even more than normal, attend all the relevant conferences and meetings, and serve on all the private/public committees you can. Although government buyers can be very tough and suspicious, in the end they have to buy from someone – make sure that someone is you by being good at what you do and very, very patient.

11 THE TROUBLE WITH RECRUITMENT

The British method (old pattern) depended on an interview in which the candidate established his identity.

Many of the problems of bureaucracy may derive from the way in which bureaucrats are recruited. In the most interesting chapter of his book (Chapter 5, The Short List, or Principles of Selection), Parkinson drew on his expertise as a historian to examine several recruitment methods that were used in the 18th and 19th centuries. According to him, before the civil service reforms in the mid-19th century, British government agencies recruited people according to the degree to which they were related to powerful aristocrats – for example, the son of a baronet would have a good chance until the nephew of a duke applied, and so on.

DEFINING IDEA

Britain has invented a new missile. It's called the civil servant – it doesn't work and it can't be fired

GENERAL SIR WALTER WALKER, FORMER NATO COMMANDER

Although this method was elitist and far from meritocratic, it was widespread across the world in pre-modern times, when the power of government was generally far shakier than it is now and depended upon ties of loyalty and land ownership. Since the explosion of industrialisation during the 19th century and the massive increase in population across the world and, finally, the effects of two shattering world wars, many countries have rejected political systems based on hereditary monarchy and nobility, and their bureaucracies have become professionalised. Nevertheless, you do still see something like the old system in the Arabian Gulf monarchies, where the top bureaucratic posts do go to members of the ruling families.

In some countries, however, a kind of 'civil service nobility' has grown up, according to some sociologists. In France, for example, it is very hard to become a senior civil servant unless you have studied at one of a handful of *grandes écoles*, to which only 1 in 20 applicants are successful. The rewards of success are great: many French ministers have been graduates of a *grande école*, and 65% of the value of companies listed on the Paris stock exchange (i.e. the biggest firms) are run by *grande école* graduates. Similarly, in Spain, recruitment into the top ranks of the civil service is done by competitive examination and many of these people go on to ministerial positions or directorships in large firms. On the face of it this seems meritocratic, since it is based on a very tough examination system, but according to the sociologist critics, top civil servants in these countries are often related to one another, probably because the examination system is consciously or unconsciously weighted towards those in the know – in other words, if you grow up in a family that understands deeply how the recruitment system works, you are more likely to succeed in the competitive examinations.

HERE'S AN IDEA FOR YOU

Worried about where your kids are going to university? If they are good students, don't be put off by the posh reputation of Oxford and Cambridge – these universities bend over backwards to give every promising applicant a fair chance, whatever their background. Competition is tough, and only about 1 in 4 applicants get accepted, but the days when they let in people because of who their relatives were are long gone.

12 FROM LOYALTY TIES TO BUREAUCRACY

The Chinese method (old pattern) was at one time so extensively copied that few people realise its origin. This is the method of Competitive Examination.

It sounds amazing, but it is true. In the 7th century AD a system of recruiting imperial officials (the mandarins) was created in China whereby any male, whatever their social status, could have a chance of success through taking exams. The exams were so hard, and it took so long to study for them, that in practice most of the applicants were from the land-owning class, but many very poor men were able, with colossal effort, to pass the exams and gain high positions.

DEFINING IDEA

A career in politics is no preparation for government.

YES MINISTER TV SERIES

It is thought that this system was developed in order to maintain the loyalty of the provinces which might otherwise have tried to break away. Government positions were distributed according to quotas, so that every province produced a number of officials in proportion to its population. It also helped to preserve a standardised Chinese culture, since everyone who entered the exams had to spend many years studying the Chinese literary classics. Another benefit was that it was in some ways a more meritocratic system – only very studious and intelligent people could pass all the exams, so it tended to keep rich but unintelligent people out of the top bureaucratic jobs, which was perhaps an improvement on earlier selection systems.

When the Europeans began to gain access to China in the early 17th century, news of the competitive examination system began to spread.

For example, Burton's *The Anatomy of Melancholy* of 1621 mentions it with approval, and throughout the 17th century many European writers suggested that the system should be adopted in their own countries. Not surprisingly, perhaps, it took more than 200 years for these suggestions to be implemented.

In 1855 a commission was set up to propose reforms for the British civil service, which had been violently attacked by the press for incompetence during the Crimean War. One of the main complaints was that civil servants had been given jobs through favouritism, not because of their ability. John Stuart Mill, the philosopher, told the government that the effect that recruitment by examination 'is calculated to produce in raising both the character of the public administration and the people can scarcely be overestimated.' By this time Europeans were less starry-eyed about the mandarin bureaucracy in China (which had become nightmarishly corrupt and inefficient) and had realised, as Mill said, that even selection by exam could lead to a 'pedantocracy'. However, it was hoped that in the British Empire an independently minded, highly intelligent and well-educated civil service could be created and maintained indefinitely. Something approaching this ideal was established, and maintained with some success from the late 19th century to the 1930s.

HERE'S AN IDEA FOR YOU

Now that the utility companies have been privatised, they appear to be applying their considerable bureaucratic talents to poaching each other's customers, using aggressive sales methods and forms of sharp practice that have not been seen in the UK for many years. For example, there is some evidence that some companies have transferred substantial numbers of former customers back to their service without the customers' knowledge. If the customer notices, the company then explains that it was an 'erroneous transfer'. Watch out!

13 FIT FOR PURPOSE?

It was considered that classical learning and literary ability would fit any candidate for any administrative post ...

Following the Northcote-Trevelyan report of 1854, the British civil service was reformed to have a kind of caste system: there would be clerks to do the routine work and a higher echelon of policymakers. The higher echelon was generally recruited from the top universities (then Oxford and Cambridge) and were chosen as brilliant generalists; as Parkinson says, many of them were selected on the basis of their excellence at Greek and Latin, especially in their ability to compose verse in the style of ancient authors, a very challenging skill.

DEFINING IDEA

Reorganizing the civil service is like drawing a knife through a bowl of marbles.

YES MINISTER, TV SERIES

By the end of World War II, there was a feeling that this system was wildly out of date. A brilliant Oxbridge-educated classicist might have been quite good at coping with imperial problems in the late 19th century, but how could he – and it was still generally a 'he' – make informed decisions in a world that was being rapidly transformed by science and technology? What was needed was a new, scientifically minded civil service that could cope with the modern world. In 1968 the Fulton report criticised the amateurishness of the civil service, and called for scientists, engineers, economists and other experts to be given more power – only they, with their special expertise, could be relied on to make the decisions the country needed to keep up with the rapid pace of technological change. Writers like C.P. Snow and politicians like Harold Wilson talked about the 'white heat' of technology that was going to transform Britain.

Half a century on, it is clear that these ideas did not have a great impact on the civil service. A few cosmetic reforms were made, but technocrats did not really come to rule the roost. Then in the 1980s and 1990s, a new version, this time based on financial efficiency and public accountability, became all the rage. A host of initiatives, from 'total quality management' and the 'Citizens Charter' to 'joined-up policy-making' came and went, none of which seems to have had a very profound effect. Now the experts are saying that the whole notion that you can turn policy implementation into a super-efficient process directed by scientifically trained experts is flawed – human nature, as it operates within bureaucracies, has to be taken into account.

We don't seem any closer to discovering what kind of person makes the perfect administrator, but perhaps the answer depends on the times. Recruiting classically educated generalists was a definite improvement on the nepotistic system that preceded it, but the system had to adapt to the pace of technological change in the 20th century. No doubt it will have to change again and again in the future.

HERE'S AN IDEA FOR YOU

If you are worried about the emergence of a Big Brother state that uses technology to know everything about us, perhaps you should relax a little. Police states are police states, whether or not they have the latest technology. And although shambling democracies like Britain have their scary Kafkaesque sides, but there isn't much evidence that their public administrations can, or ever will, develop the competence to control people to that extent.

14 LOOKISM

Heaped on the table before this committee are 483 forms of application, with testimonials attached ... Some have attached their photographs. Others have (perhaps wisely) refrained from doing so.

DEFINING IDEA

Politics is just show business for ugly people.

JAY LENO, TV HOST

Here Parkinson, in the days before political correctness, makes a passing reference to the phenomenon where applicants are rejected because of their unappealing appearance. This is 'lookism', or prejudice against people who are not good looking.

Is lookism just another bit of political correctness gone mad? Not really; the evidence for the effect is quite strong. Most of us have a vague idea that good-looking people seem to be more successful at certain things. Social scientists have now had some success in measuring the phenomenon. For example, although ideas of beauty vary between cultures, studies show that they are actually quite standardised within particular cultures for quite long periods of time, according to studies that ask people to rank a selection of photos of men and women according to their looks. These standards don't last forever, though: back in the 1890s companies in Europe and the US were marketing food for weight gain to prevent 'the shame of a poor, thin figure' (just as they still do in the Far East), while today everyone in the West seems obsessed with losing weight.

Men who are generally perceived as ugly on average earn about 9% less than average in the US, while the best-looking earn 5% more than the average. Good-looking male lawyers become partners in their law firms more quickly, and are able to charge more for their services. They are also more likely to appear in court and to run their own practices, both of which are activities that involve giving a good impression to strangers.

Interestingly, the impact of this kind of unconscious discrimination seems to be less for women. Plain women, for instance, seem to earn only 4% less than the average. Looks don't seem to have an effect on whether or not a woman marries, according to the studies, but plain women are more likely to marry less well-educated men.

People want to have more social contact with good-looking people, and are more likely to co-operate with them. Good-looking men are more likely to co-operate with other people than are ugly men, while in contrast, good-looking women are less likely to co-operate with others than are plain women.

Clearly, the phenomenon of lookism cannot be ignored. Probably it goes very deep – as well as the cultural norms, there aspects of lookism that have a 'primitive', biological basis, and can probably never been rooted out of recruitment processes entirely, however unfair they may be.

HERE'S AN IDEA FOR YOU

What do you think of your own looks? According to the latest research, your self-perception has a measurable effect on your career success. People whom others do not rate as very good looking, but who rate themselves as very good looking, are more successful than people who rate themselves in line with the ratings of others. So maybe all those make-over shows and the explosion in cosmetic surgery are worthwhile after all – you may not be able to make a silk purse out of a sow's ear, but the better you can make yourself feel about your own looks, the more successful you are likely to be.

15 COUNTRIES ARE RUN BY THE WISE?

Solemn conclaves of the wise and good are mere figments of the teacher's mind.

We are taught at school to think of the bodies and institutions that run our world as being sensible, well informed and able to respond well to new challenges. This takes a half a lifetime to unlearn, and to realise that top decision-makers, especially when they are working in groups, frequently devise schemes that go dreadfully wrong.

DEFINING IDEA

Government is not a team. It is a loose confederation of warring tribes.

YES MINISTER TV SERIES

A good example of this is 'e-government' (electronic government). Back in the 1990s, when the internet took off and dotcom companies were booming, the US government began to think that it might be a good idea to take advantage of the web to increase efficiency and productivity. This wasn't a bad idea. Soon, the fabulously named Government Paperwork Elimination Act was passed, which was designed to allow citizens to submit forms online instead of on paper. Trendier academics started to rave about the fantastic benefits that would accrue: e-government was going to empower the public, make government more efficient, and transform bureaucracy into a responsive, forward-thinking powerhouse that would help usher in the new information age in what was called a 'paradigm shift'. In 2000, Bill Clinton announced that e-government was going to drastically reduce red tape and make the country even more democratic.

Soon, other countries were following suit. Everyone seemed to have an e-government programme that was going to decentralise, cut costs and generally make the world a better place. In the more technologically advanced countries, this has to some extent been successful. In the US, the UK and Singapore, for instance, routine chores like renewing driving licences and passports can now be done a bit faster and easier online than it used to take using 'snail mail'. There were plenty of hiccups, but a decade on most of us are used to dealing with the bureaucrats through the internet, which at the very least has to be better than waiting to see them in their dreary offices.

In the developing world, however, the picture is less rosy. These countries too, remember, generally have well-educated, sophisticated people running their bureaucracies, at least at the higher levels. They saw e-government as a chance for massive bureaucratic reform and modernisation. But now, a few years on, 85% of e-government projects in developing countries have been partial or total failures, according to the World Bank. One of the major problems is said to be that departments are possessive and resist co-operating with other departments on e-government projects; in other words, they are instinctively react against e-government's threat to existing hierarchical structures. Case studies of failures in Asia, Africa and Latin America highlight this problem: projects failed because they 'threatened existing privileges', were 'deliberately undermined' by certain offices, fell afoul of 'political rivalries', were 'resisted by senior officials', or were simply obstructed by staff who 'were reluctant to alter their existing work patterns'. In these confrontations between 'the wise and the good' and bureaucracy, it seems, bureaucracy is winning.

HERE'S AN IDEA FOR YOU

No project can stay on track without using clear performance measures to check progress. But measuring performance won't work unless everyone has agreed on the performance measures beforehand – so take the trouble to hammer out the details of how the progress of the project will be evaluated before you begin.

16 THE ENDLESS DRIVE TO REMOVE BIAS

The formula 'reject everyone over 50 or under 20 plus everyone who is Irish' is now universally used.

DEFINING IDEA

All of us do not have equal talent, but all of us should have an equal opportunity to develop our talents.
JOHN F. KENNEDY

In Parkinson's day, the idea that people should have equal opportunities had not yet become established. But why, in these more enlightened times, are we still so obsessed with equal opportunity?

Equal opportunity is actually a political idea that presupposes that the socio-economic strata in society cannot be done away with. The aim is not to create total quality, but to give people from all parts of society an equal chance of obtaining a desirable job or social position. That's in strong contrast to many ancient societies, for instance, where your future often depended upon what caste or social group you were born into.

That all seems straightforward, but if you look more closely you find that equal opportunity takes many forms, some of which are in conflict with one another. Take the case of Singapore and Malaysia, which became a single independent state in 1963. Singapore, an island city that had a predominantly ethnically Chinese population, argued strongly that the new state should have equality for all its citizens, but was over-ruled by the Malaysian government, who implemented a policy of favouring the 'Bumiputra' (sons of the soil), who were mainly ethnic Malays, over other ethnic groups. While Malays saw the Bumiputra policy as a kind of positive discrimination for ethnic Malays who had been to some extent disadvantaged in colonial times, Singaporeans wanted a society based on meritocracy.

Singapore was expelled from Malaysia in 1965 and became an independent state. The new country was now in a position to practice what it had preached about equality. In some ways it has achieved this aim, but the government's obsession with using academic achievement as the main criterion for promotion, according to some observers, is creating a society of rigid castes governed by a narrow-minded elite.

Singapore represents an interesting experiment in removing one kind of bias, only to have unwittingly created another. Across the world, although there are now strong movements – in many cases supported by legislation – to remove various biases from recruitment, many more biases still remain and new ones are created. We may be trying to prevent ourselves from recruiting on grounds of race, gender, or sexual orientation, but there are other, subtler biases.

One recent study examined whether managers unconsciously use stereotypes when recruiting, and also whether they favour certain demographic groups over others. The results showed that older people found it the hardest to get hired, and that young women were the group that found it the easiest. Young male managers avoided hiring young men, and older managers avoided hiring older men. Older women tended to hire older women, who otherwise were the most discriminated group. Overall, it was quite plain that many firms had a cult of youth, believing that it is better to hire younger people.

HERE'S AN IDEA FOR YOU

All of us age, and eventually have to confront ageism. Here are a few ways to beat the bias: keep fit; have some young friends as well as older ones; go for activities where experience counts; learn new skills.

17 THE HIDDEN JOB MARKET

The great thing is that all the applications are thrown into the wastepaper basket, only one applicant being considered, and he a man who did not apply.

When you hear about the extraordinary number of applications employers sometimes receive when they advertise jobs, you can't help wondering if they throw their carefully devised selection processes out of the window and just pick someone they already know. In the quotation above, Parkinson is talking about the selection procedures for university lecturers in the Far East during the 1950s. Of course, selecting someone for an academic job is a process that is hard to systematise because it is so subjective. Candidate X for the job of biology lecturer may have all the right qualifications, but Candidate Y, the discoverer of a rare type of crane fly, has that extra zing … in the eyes of some members of the selection committee, but not others. Perhaps deciding, for instance, which candidate is best for the job of telemarketing consultant is a little easier to make into a formal, 'objective' system involving checklists and box ticking.

DEFINING IDEA
Speak to those who are already predisposed to want what you offer.
STEVE PAVLINA, BUSINESS WRITER

The truth is, though, that many people obtain employment without having to go through a formalised competitive process. You often see the statistic quoted that only 20% of jobs are ever advertised openly; the rest of the positions are said to be filled through other means, by way of the 'hidden job market'.

Is there really a hidden job market and, if so, does anybody really know how big it is? Yes, there really is one, in the sense that many employers, especially in smaller firms, find it easier and more convenient to employ people without advertising. Think about it from the employer's point of view. Suppose you are running a small firm employing three people and you need an office assistant. What's easier, advertise and then go through a tiresome and expensive selection process, or ask people you know if they know of anyone who would like the job? If you hire that person and find that they are keen and able, you may be happy to promote them as your firm grows. Or suppose you are running a software-writing department. If someone from another firm, whom you know to be talented and likeable, says that she would like to work for you, wouldn't it be easier just to hire them instead of advertising?

Of course, larger employers are generally required by law to go through a more formal process, but even then there are 'hidden' vacancies. Some positions are only advertised internally. Some start out as short-term contracts to outside consultants and get turned into permanent positions because the firm likes the person they hired.

HERE'S AN IDEA FOR YOU

When you are networking, don't just go around with a wan smile asking everyone you meet for a job. Look for information – about the industry, about firms, about the rivalries and alliances between people (who are often working in different firms). Figuring out who is looking for what you have to offer is the key – don't just blunder around without knowing who you are talking to: work out who is able and willing to help you.

18 PSYCHOLOGICAL TESTS

Modern myths centre upon the intelligence test and the psychological interview.

We may have got better at understanding what they mean, but the intelligence test and the psychological interview (and tests) remain an integral part of many large employers' recruitment process. The IQ tests, notoriously flawed though they are, perhaps deliver something worth knowing about the applicant. The same ought to be true of personality tests, but it is much easier to cheat.

DEFINING IDEA

Do not employ handsome servants.
CHINESE PROVERB

For example, in the US some retailers use personality tests to hire people working in their shops. The personality tests they use, naturally, are not designed to identify high-fliers but people who fit a predetermined profile for a shop attendant. With a bit of detective work, it is possible to discover what the 'right' answers are.

The questions also include items that seem biased towards US cultural norms; for example, you may be asked to agree or disagree with the statement, 'You have to give up on some things that you start.' The right answer, apparently, is 'Strongly disagree.' Well, if you were trying to hire talented business people, you might decide that 'strongly agree' would be a more appropriate answer, since in high-risk activities you often have to give up on some initiatives and cut your losses. But no, shop attendants are expected never to give up on anything they undertake! Perhaps the rationale is that shop attendants are unlikely ever to be required to undertake anything particularly risky or difficult, and therefore they should never give up …

This is the Big Brother mentality writ large. It's all about second-guessing people's mentalities, however complex they may be in reality. Its main advantage, as far as the company is concerned, appears to be that it screens a large number of applicants automatically, and reduces the number of people that have to be interviewed. That would be fine if the process screened out the worst applicants – and some companies claim that it does, pointing to lower staff turnover since they introduced the test. However, since many firms allow people to apply again for other jobs (and take the same test), and since many firms use similar tests, it is possible with practice to figure out enough of the 'right' answers to get through the screening process.

Various studies have looked at the effectiveness of personality tests at predicting future behaviour. They have found, for instance, that graphology tests (used by many French companies) are very poor predictors. The best method appears to be that used by professionally run 'assessment centres' that administer a battery of tests, group work and interviews that measure a whole range of different abilities, from spatial awareness to emotional stability, and are judged by industrial psychologists who actually know what they are doing. That's what large organisations like the civil service use as part of their extremely lengthy recruitment process – it's a world away from the firms that use a single test as a primitive screen for job applicants.

HERE'S AN IDEA FOR YOU

Don't worry about the tests – practise them! There are plenty of sample tests available, and there is strong evidence that the more you practice them, the better you are likely to perform on the real ones.

19 THE CAUTIOUS BUREAUCRAT

The persons who satisfy this type of examiner are usually of a cautious and suspicious temperament, pedantic and sly, saying little and doing nothing.

Here Parkinson was criticising a method of recruitment where candidates were invited to a country house for a weekend and carefully observed by the recruiters. These days, this is done at assessment centres, but HR assessment techniques have improved since Parkinson's time, and a really sly, cautious person would probably have to fake enthusiastic assertiveness to have any hope of being selected.

DEFINING IDEA

Cautious, careful people, always casting about to preserve their reputations ... can never effect a reform.
SUSAN B. ANTHONY, 19TH CENTURY CIVIL RIGHTS ACTIVIST

Nevertheless, we've all encountered the type. One famous actress is remembered by people who were fellow students with her at university as being 'the kind of person who, when someone said something funny, would wait to see who laughed before she laughed herself.' And bureaucracy seems to be particularly attractive to this kind of person.

To understand why and how people operate like this, we should consider 'game theory', a mathematical discipline that sheds light on competing strategies and is widely applied in many disciplines, from evolutionary biology to political science. In game theory, such a person could be regarded as adopting a specific, consistent strategy. The success of any particular strategy will depend on the rules of the game irrespective of whatever moral value we may ascribe to it, according to the theory. In a highly competitive, aggressive game, for example, a cautious strategy will not do well, but nor will a highly aggressive strategy that never backs down: both will eventually be brought down by another competitor. In such a game, a strategy of only retaliating when someone attacks, but otherwise being co-operative, turns out to be the optimal method.

What kind of game do bureaucracies play? And should we believe them when they say they are trying to become more efficient and business-like? Many expert observers believe that bureaucracies, especially in the public sector, still play a game that favours a cautious strategy above all. According to evidence given by Nick Birks, a senior civil servant, to the UK Parliament's Public Administration Committee in 2010, 'civil servants are incentivised for adherence to process and avoidance of risk, not pursuit of outcomes' and 'find it difficult to step outside of a role in which they have been successful and may have a subconscious interest in preserving the status quo, in which they know how to perform well, even when the environment has changed.'

HERE'S AN IDEA FOR YOU

Despite all the complaints, there is no doubt that many very intelligent, able people work for the UK civil service, but this is not the case in many other countries. If you think that you will get the same treatment abroad as you do in the UK, you may be in for a shock. In Greece, for example, about a quarter of the working population are in the civil service, and, according to the NGO, Transparency International, corruption is rife. So if you're thinking of going abroad to buy a holiday home, retire, or start a business, take a long hard look at the government bureaucracy there: they may turn out to be your worst headache.

20 IS MANAGEMENT THEORY A WASTE OF TIME?

Intermingled with volumes about ape men and spaceships, these textbooks would harm no one.

Parkinson asserted that books on theories of business management and public administration were works of fiction that bear little relation to the reality of how bureaucracies work. But in the last few decades, there has

been a massive increase in management education – in the US alone, the number of people earning business degrees each year has more than quadrupled since the 1970s, and business schools have been popping up like mushrooms all over the world, from Nigeria to Bangladesh. Surely this reflects the improvement in our understanding of how to manage bureaucracy?

Maybe not. Let's consider NASA, the US space agency, which has an annual budget of some $187 billion a year, and is at the forefront of a wide range of cutting-edge research and technology. One might expect that any lessons that have been learned about managing bureaucracy during the half-century since NASA's foundation in 1958 would have been incorporated into an organisation that is the epitome of the modern age. Yet an official investigation into the space shuttle *Columbia* disaster of 2003, when the spacecraft disintegrated on its return to the earth, found that organisational problems were a major factor in NASA's failure to prevent the tragedy.

These problems included poor communication between different teams within NASA, poor leadership, and a failure to implement formal procedures. The investigation also found these problems had been identified after an earlier disaster, the explosion of the space shuttle *Challenger* in 1986. Although attempts were made to resolve the issues after *Challenger*, they had re-emerged 17 years later in the *Columbia* disaster. Since 2003, a large number of writers have attempted to analyse and cure NASA's organisational problems. Authors William H. Starbuck and Moshe Farjoun argue that 'NASA has responded to problems by adding layers rather than by clarifying', commenting that 'to attempt to manage NASA must be extremely frustrating'. That's pure Parkinson!

One of the current fashions in management theory is 'change management', which is supposed to show organisations how they can transform themselves into more desirable states, such as becoming a 'learning organisation'. But there's plenty of evidence that failure rates are very high; according to some studies, as much as 70% of 'change initiatives' fail to achieve their goals. Well, at least it keeps all the management consultants and business school academics in work.

HERE'S AN IDEA FOR YOU

Has the challenge of change management got you stumped? When Jurgen Weber, the boss of Germany's state-owned airline Lufthansa, realised that the firm was on the point of bankruptcy in 1992, he decided to take a dramatic approach. Holding meetings with four different groups of 50 managers each, he took them through the details of the crisis and delivered an ultimatum: 'either you come up with ways we can get out of this, or I'll shut the company down'. Weber and the 200 managers then went out to the employees, and repeated the process in hundreds of meetings. The result? By discussing the crisis openly and inclusively, Weber was able get the co-operation of workers and unions, and successfully implemented cost-cutting measures that saved the company.

21 SECRETS

Students of social science must keep this information to themselves and members of the general public are not on any account to read it.

Max Weber, the great sociologist, believed that bureaucracies are naturally secretive about what they know, what they do and what their objectives are. According to him they do this to retain an advantage over others; if people don't know what a bureaucracy is doing, then they cannot criticise it effectively or do much to change it. This applies both to government bureaucracies and bureaucratic units within other organisations, such as commercial firms. Often there is a plausible reason for the secrecy – the Official Secrets Act, for instance, or rules on personal confidentiality within a human resources department. The trouble is that a necessary and legitimate rule on confidentiality (such as that we don't really want enemy countries to know our military secrets) can easily be used as a screen to hide behind.

DEFINING IDEA

If people don't know what you're doing, they don't know what you're doing wrong.

YES MINISTER, TV SERIES

The way that officialdom, both in central government and in local government, hides behind secrecy rules is so obvious and ever-present that it hardly needs to be examined further. But it is also surprisingly common in commercial organisations. One of the big issues in the management of multinational firms, for instance, is the problem of 'silos'. Organisational 'silos' are units within a firm that have a function – for example, product design or delivery – that do not communicate well with other units. For example, it is surprisingly common for engineers within a firm to design products that the manufacturing unit subsequently explains are impossible to make; or for buyers to try to save money by buying poor-quality materials that, much later, turn out to have severely reduced the quality of a finished product. Often this poor communication is the result of a bureaucratic, not-invented-here attitude within one of the silos.

Almost all types of organisation now use techniques discovered by social scientists in order to manipulate or influence people's behaviour. These techniques work a lot better if the people at whom they are targeted don't know exactly what is happening. Arranging products in supermarkets to encourage impulse buying, putting a touch of baby powder through the air conditioning in Las Vegas casinos to encourage older people to gamble more (this really works!) and the constant barrage of 'public information' campaigns are all examples of methods that rely to some degree on deception – and secrecy – to reach optimum effectiveness. For instance, there have been a number of confessional TV talk shows that use the device of administering a lie-detector test to check whether or not a guest on the show is lying. Viewers are left with the impression that the results of the lie-detector test are reliable; many people do not know that lie-detectors are in fact quite unreliable, especially if the person being tested knows this – in other words, people who know that lie-detectors are unreliable are more likely to be able to generate misleading readings! We need to recognise that bureaucracies of all kinds are using such techniques to try to influence us, and it's not always in our best interests to go along with it.

HERE'S AN IDEA FOR YOU

Don't take information you receive from any organisation, even the government, on trust. Much of the time it has been doctored, often with good intentions, to create a bias. The solution? Get on the internet and do your own research.

22 COMITOLOGY

It would be unsound to conclude … that the science of comitology is in an advanced state of development.

Parkinson coined the term 'comitology' as a joke, to mean the scientific study of committees and their behaviour – the idea that people might study committee behaviour seemed vaguely ridiculous to him at the time. He would have roared with laughter to discover that, 50 years later, the European Community had reinvented the word to mean not the study of committees, but of what committees do – i.e. the meetings they have to deliberate on such weighty matters as changing or implementing community laws, directives, regulations and rules, and advancing community policies. It also refers to the fantastically complex system of some 250 committees and subcommittees, all with different powers, that exist within the European Community and which interact with member states, the European Parliament and the European Commission. It's a bureaucrat's dream come true!

DEFINING IDEA

I have always found the word 'Europe' on the lips of those who wanted something from others which they dared not demand in their own names.

OTTO VON BISMARCK,
GERMAN CHANCELLOR, 1880.

The comitology committees work like miniature councils of ministers. They meet in Brussels and vote on their decisions. Originally set up in the 1960s as a way for member states to keep an eye on European Union law-making, some of the committees have become a battleground between different groups of civil servants vying for influence, while others, according to researchers, have become autonomous entities that reach decisions by general consensus but whose members do not represent the interests of the member states who appointed them – this is known by the compelling phrase 'bureaucratic drift'.

'Bureaucratic drift' happens when a group of people in a sub-organisation – like a committee – begin to break away from the chain of command and to make decisions without the guidance, knowledge or approval of their superiors. According to numerous studies, the way in which the complex network of expert advisors, European civil servants and national civil servants arrive at detailed decisions is not properly overseen either by national governments or by the European Commission. National parliaments and opposition parties find it extremely difficult to discover the details of the activities of these committees. According to a recent House of Lords report, much of the legislation that is produced by the comitology committees is not properly scrutinised by national governments at all; in effect, some of the committees, largely made up of civil servants from member-state governments, have become unaccountable for their decisions.

Perhaps these committees are making good decisions. Perhaps the people who sit on them are the best people for the job, with the most expertise and the right experience. But if even the member states' governments can't find out what they are doing, it's hardly a sign that this great political experiment – a voluntary federation of sovereign states – has mastered the art of keeping its bureaucracy in control. As far as the EU is concerned, Parkinson's assessment of 'comitology' still holds true.

HERE'S AN IDEA FOR YOU

Love it or hate it, we have to live with the EU, so why not engage with it? The EU publishes a vast amount of information on the internet, and the forthcoming European Citizens' Initiative promises to provide a means of 'direct democracy', by allowing EU citizens to petition for legislation that they themselves propose. Don't leave it all to the bureaucrats: participate!

23 HOW TO WASTE TIME AT MEETINGS

The time spent on any item of the agenda will be in inverse proportion to the sum involved.

Parkinson thought that committee meetings tended to waste a lot of time on unimportant issues because many of the members didn't understand the big, important items on the agenda and seized on the small items as ways of showing that they could make a contribution. The solution to the problem that Parkinson identifies is to train participants to be effective, and only to invite those who are actually needed at the meeting. The next problem is: do you have the power to introduce such a training programme?

DEFINING IDEA
When you go to meetings or auditions and you fail to prepare, prepare to fail.
PAULA ABDUL, SINGER AND ACTRESS

According to Intel, the computer chip manufacturer, careful training in how to hold meetings is the answer. Andy Grove, the famous founder of Intel, thinks that there are two kinds of meetings: the 'process meeting', which are held regularly to exchange information, and the 'mission meeting', which are held to deal with a specific, stand-alone issue. In order to make meetings more efficient, Grove set up a variety of training programmes to educate employees in holding meetings. New employees attend an 'effective meetings' session to learn how to define the aim of any meeting, how to draw up a sensible agenda and, very importantly, how to decide who should actually attend the meeting. Outside contractors, such as consultants, must also attend a training course in facilitating meetings that focus on issues such as how to keep the meeting on course and how to 'break the ice' so that people attending a meeting participate appropriately.

Intel sees two key issues as central to holding efficient meetings: is the meeting necessary? (or, for example, can it be done by email?), and, if a decision has to be made, are the right decision-makers going to be present? In 'mission meetings', which are generally held to draw up a plan or make a specific decision, the company believes that there is usually one person who is more committed to achieving a firm outcome than anyone else. Intel thinks that this person should be the 'chairman', and that he or she should work hard before the meeting to lay the groundwork, for example by consulting with colleagues about the feasibility of aspects of the plan.

It is vital to make sure that people are only invited to meetings if they are really needed. For example, some people attend as many meetings as possible just as a way to get some 'me' time where they can write their diaries, check their personal emails on their laptops, or plan their dinner parties while people chat away. Of course, an organisation that allows this to happen – or doesn't know that it is happening – is being badly managed.

HERE'S AN IDEA FOR YOU

You can't hold effective meetings without a clear agenda. Prepare it well in advance, include an estimate of how long the meeting will take, and design the topics so that you can have a structured discussion that leads to a clearly defined outcome. Finally, circulate the agenda to all the participants long before the meeting is held. They'll appreciate the effort!

24 THE MEANING OF FANCY OFFICES

You are ankle deep in the director's carpet, plodding sturdily towards his distant, tidy desk. Hypnotised by the chief's unwavering stare, cowed by the Matisse hung up on his wall, you will feel that you have found real efficiency at last.

Having unbelievably luxurious offices is nothing new – remember all those fabulous art-deco offices from the 1930s? According to Parkinson, an impressive office has an overpowering effect on people who visit it; its wealth, modernity and size are designed to make visitors believe in the organisation's invincibility – but, argued Parkinson, it's all an illusion.

DEFINING IDEA

All that glisters is not gold ... Gilded tombs do worms enfold

WILLIAM SHAKESPEARE. *THE MERCHANT OF VENICE*

Organisations that create plush offices do so for a number of reasons. Perhaps the most important is to overawe customers and suppliers. When you walk into a really plush office, like the one Parkinson describes, that is more expensively decorated than any palace or fancy hotel, you receive a strong impression of wealth and success. Perhaps this will make you more willing to do business with such an organisation. Companies that have trouble distinguishing themselves from their competitors, such as the top law firms, or that are in the business of selling, such as advertising agencies, often create amazingly fancy offices for this reason. Their real business – reading contracts and coming up with silly ideas – is hidden away because it is difficult to make that look glamorous.

Then there are the firms that want to create the impression that they are richer and more successful than they really are. In this case, the fancy office is meant to convey somehow the impression that the firm (and by implication, you the customer) have discovered a route to easy money. You often see this happening in a particular company, industry or location that is enjoying a dangerous boom that is likely to be followed by a collapse. For example, Enron, the gigantic energy company that went spectacularly bankrupt in 2001 because of accounting fraud, had fabulous offices across the world, replete with the most expensive office chairs, the latest computer technology, gyms, lifts with glass surrounds, and held massive parties for its thousands of employees – all at a time when insiders were busily recording fictitious profits to pay for all the opulence.

Dubai looks like the latest example of this phenomenon. This tiny Gulf state went through an extraordinary building boom as the country made a bold effort to switch from an oil-based trading economy to one based on tourism and services. Artificial islands peppered with deluxe condominium buildings sprang up along its coast to attract the newly rich from all over the world. But the international financial crisis hit it badly in 2008, property collapsed, and it had to get bailed out by its neighbour, Abu Dhabi. Dubai will survive the crisis, no doubt, and we should perhaps applaud the emirate's brave attempt to transform itself in the face of a very uncertain future. But let's not kid ourselves: turning your country into a giant flashy shopping mall is no guarantee of long-term survival.

HERE'S AN IDEA FOR YOU

Flashy, imposing premises may indeed be an important indicator – but not necessarily – of the true health of the organisation. The next time you encounter them, ask yourself: what is the intended effect, and what does the glitz really hide?

25 MEGAPROJECTS

It is now known that a perfection of planned layout is achieved only by institutions on the point of collapse.

DEFINING IDEA

And Babylon shall become heaps, a dwelling place for dragons, an astonishment, and an hissing, without an inhabitant.

THE BIBLE, JEREMIAH 51:37

Although Parkinson is exaggerating for humorous effect, in the world of infrastructure development, increasingly ambitious projects are indeed causing major headaches for their sponsors.

Recent work by Danish scientist Professor Bent Flyvbjerg has sparked a lively debate on the poor performance of 'megaprojects', the huge, multi-billion dollar infrastructure projects that, Flyvbjerg says, have sharply increased in number across the world in recent years and 'are central to the new politics of distance'. Despite the financial crisis that began in 2007, the megaproject business is booming, especially in the developing world. In terms of the percentage of their GDP, megaproject spending in some countries, such as China and India, is beating all records, even of the massive infrastructure investment in Europe during the 19th century. All over the world, newly industrialised countries are spending trillions on roads, bridges, airports and power plants that are intended to provide the framework for future economic growth.

Clearly, building more infrastructure is important. Improvements in transport, for example, can boost business productivity and create jobs very rapidly. Farms in remote places can suddenly gain access to export markets simply because they can get their produce to ports quickly.

Better water improves health and thus releases more people into a growing labour market. Urbanisation, combined with new jobs, creates new domestic consumer markets. However, according to Flyvbjerg, many such projects suffer from appalling problems: they cost much more and earn much less than estimated; the public are deliberately kept away from the decision-making process; and the environmental impact is overlooked. Cost overruns average about 50% across all projects, but in extreme cases can cost many times the original estimate – for example, the Sydney Opera House, which cost 15 times more, and Concorde, which cost 12 times more.

We can't put these problems down solely to bureaucratic incompetence in the public sector since even when the private sector invests significantly in a megaproject, as in the case of the Channel Tunnel, the problems occur. According to some widely accepted studies, the UK would have been better off economically if the Chunnel had never been built.

The boffins haven't come up with a complete solution to the problem, but point to two important causative factors: 'optimism bias', a human tendency to expect unrealistically good outcomes; and 'strategic misrepresentation', which means deliberately distorting information, for example in budgets, in order to move a project forward. Flyvberg thinks that if you take the incentives to lie out of megaproject planning, they'll work much better.

HERE'S AN IDEA FOR YOU

If you think waste in megaprojects can never affect you directly, consider the case of Dubai. In the noughties, Dubai went through an extraordinary boom building a series of megaprojects such as a residential project on a gigantic archipelago of artificial islands in the shape of the world. Many expats bought property to avoid the high rents. Then the market crashed in 2008, and now expats are locked in a nightmare of negative equity and rising interest rates.

26 BATTLE OF THE BUREAUCRACIES

The cure, whatever its nature, must come from the outside.

Parkinson argued that moribund bureaucracies could only be reformed from the outside. But what if many bureaucracies are involved, and the organisations demanding the reform are equally past their best?

Something of this kind occurred after the World Health Organisation (WHO) mounted worldwide campaigns against bird flu in 2005/2006, and H1N1 (swine flu) in 2009, but few people died. The risks of a pandemic were real, according to virologists, and it was right to take precautions against these diseases, which might rapidly mutate into a more lethal form. The trouble is, immunising a vast number of people quickly is a tall order, costs a great deal of money, and creates a lot of work and worry for everybody. That's a small price to pay to avoid the death of millions of people, of course, but as few deaths occurred and the number of new cases of H1N1 began to decrease in late 2009, people began to wonder if it had all been an unnecessary scare.

DEFINING IDEA

When those subject to bureaucratic control seek to escape the influence of existing bureaucratic apparatus, this is normally possible only by creating an organisation of their own which is equally subject to the process of bureaucratisation.
MAX WEBER, 19TH CENTURY SOCIOLOGIST

Then, in January 2010, the Council of Europe, a pan-European über-bureaucracy distinct from the EU, claimed that the WHO had been pressured into declaring a 'false pandemic' by the major pharmaceutical companies who stood to gain from selling vaccines, and announced that it would investigate the issue. This suspicion was bolstered later by an article in the *British Medical Journal*, which suggested that some of WHO's advisers had close financial links with the pharmaceutical companies. In a Council of Europe report by backbench MP David Flynn, it was alleged, among other things, that WHO had changed its definition of a pandemic and 'lowered the threshold for its declaration' just before declaring that H1N1 was pandemic and that pharmaceutical companies were set to make $7–10 billion in one-off profits from flu vaccine sales in 2009.

WHO has defended itself convincingly from allegations of having been unduly influenced by pharmaceutical firms and has done its best to be transparent (this, of course, involves endless meetings and press conferences, and mountains of reports). In early 2011 an expert review of the global response to the pandemic exonerated WHO from any deliberate wrongdoing. In its discussion of WHO's shortcomings, however, it revealed some marvellously Parkinsonian phenomena, such as that: WHO's 'weekly requests for specific data were overwhelming to some countries'; 'WHO may have inadvertently contributed to confusion and suspicion'; and 'a multiplicity of technical units within the Organization [were] individually generating an unmanageable number of documents'.

Its recommendations? Yet more committees, more procedures, and more documents. Well, it all makes work for the bureaucrat to do!

HERE'S AN IDEA FOR YOU

When there is a scare on and bureaucracies worldwide all suddenly need something in a hurry, there are opportunities to make money fast, even for small businesses. During the H1N1 scare, sales of thermometers, vitamins, anti-bacterial soap and tissues rocketed, and there was a bonanza in advice lines – some unscrupulous clinics were offering short telephone consultations for £45 a pop.

27 INJELITITIS AT THE UN?

We find everywhere a type of organization ... in which the higher officials are plodding and dull, those less senior are active only in intrigue against each other, and the junior men are frustrated or frivolous.

'Injelititis' is Parkinson's made-up word for organisational paralysis, where a bureaucracy has become so incompetent that it is unable to do anything useful at all. Perhaps the best example of 'injelitis' today is the United Nations and its many specialised agencies, such as UNESCO and the WTO.

DEFINING IDEA

Routine is not organization, any more than paralysis is order.

SIR ARTHUR HELPS, 19TH CENTURY CIVIL SERVANT

Now, you have to be careful when analysing an international organisation that includes countries of every ideological hue, because whatever it does, someone somewhere is bound to be screaming that it is doing it wrong. And that was the *raison d'etre* for founding the UN in the first place: after the utter failure of its predecessor, the League of Nations, to prevent the outbreak of World War II, the UN was set up in 1945 with the express purpose of promoting international peace and development, in particular through dialogue between potential enemies. And if the price of world peace is to create a bloated bureaucracy with a huge number of sinecures, it's surely a small price to pay.

During the Cold War period, when the possibility of a third World War seemed very real, that argument had a lot of force. And, even today, many politicians argue that the UN remains the least-bad solution to the problem of trying to maintain world peace. Recently, however, there has been an increasing number of claims from UN insiders that the organisation is becoming useless and irrelevant. Take, for example, Inga-Britt Ahlenius, the Under-Secretary-General for the United Nations Office of Internal Oversight Services between 2005 and 2010, who at the end of her term of office wrote to the Secretary General asserting that the UN Secretariat (the UN's huge central bureaucracy) had 'no transparency', lacked accountability, strong leadership and good governance, and that the UN as a whole was 'in a process of decline' and is 'seen less and less as a relevant partner in the resolution of world problems'.

Maybe we can dismiss Ms. Ahlenius's report as just a case of one stuffy bureaucrat scolding another, but what about Mark Malloch Brown, a former UN Deputy Secretary-General, who says that 'people are looking around the UN to build coalitions on the side' and that the UN 'has had difficulty in reflecting the shifts in today's power'? Or Jean-Pierre Lehmann, professor of international political economy at Lausanne, who thinks that 'the UN has been a terrible disappointment ... which serves as a gravy train for a very bloated employment system, and, yes, there is huge overlap between the agencies'?

HERE'S AN IDEA FOR YOU

What can be done about organisations suffering from injelititis? Parkinson thought that the only solution was for really able people to pretend to be incompetent on their way to the top, and only reveal their dynamism once they had got there. More recently, management theorists have argued that breaking up businesses into much smaller independent units can give them a new lease of life. Giving managers the incentives to perform outstandingly, so the thinking goes, will galvanise them into action.

28 BREAKING BARRIERS BETWEEN ORGANISATIONS

An exchange of ideas and personnel is a good thing – although to be sure, the few men we have had from Toprank have been rather disappointing. We can only expect the people they have thrown out.

Here Parkinson is writing in the voice of the boss of an organisation, called 'Lowgrade', that is suffering from 'injelititis' (see Chapter 27). The boss is complacent about the low position of the organisation in relation to others and sees no reason to change: any interaction with other firms, as far as this boss is concerned, will make no difference to the status quo.

Some successful firms, however, have transformed their businesses by breaking down the barriers between their customers, suppliers and themselves. One medium-sized manufacturer of car seat components in the US, for example, made a habit of studying the methods of its customers (car manufacturers) as closely as possible to perfect its supply and manufacturing processes. Then it purchased a number of firms making other car seat components so it could offer entire seats to its customers. As the car industry entered a period of decline, the firm was able gradually to persuade one car manufacturer to allow it to study how it designed car seats, and eventually began to design seats jointly with its customer. The result was a success, increasing profit margins for both firms, and turning their adversarial relationship into an amicable and constructive one.

DEFINING IDEA

If we do not hang together, we will all hang separately.

BENJAMIN FRANKLIN

A willingness to make proprietary information and expertise available to customers and suppliers can achieve striking gains in efficiency, leading to improved profits for all involved. In commoditised businesses, such as FMCG (Fast-Moving Consumer Goods), this strategy has been remarkably successful. One major chain store, for instance, gives its thousands of regular suppliers access to its computer system, enabling them to monitor their products' sales in real time, analyse the effects of price cuts and promotions, process ordering and invoicing, and upload inventory information – this has had a dramatic effect in reducing administrative costs and stock levels along the whole supply chain.

Some widely diversified conglomerates have gone even further, and provide teams of their own experts to selected customers to work on specific projects, often ones that are unrelated to the products and services the conglomerate sells. The idea here is that the conglomerate can provide know-how and resources the customer could not acquire easily on its own. Suppose a smallish manufacturer would like to switch some of its manufacturing to China, a notoriously difficult process, and has no idea where to start – the conglomerate, with its wide experience of this process, provides a team to help plan, research, negotiate and execute the project. If the project succeeds, the conglomerate hopes to benefit eventually from the customer's growth.

HERE'S AN IDEA FOR YOU

The potential benefits of closer co-operation with customers and/or suppliers are substantial, but such initiatives often go wrong, usually because the degree of commitment has been underestimated. If you really want to create closer relationships, you need to select the organisations carefully, know a lot about them already, and manage the process carefully. Planning a series of increasingly close collaborations over the long term, where both parties gain benefits along the way, only works if there are determined managers who 'champion' the process.

29 HOW TO INCREASE SUPPORT

Amid all this drivel the useful men present, if there are any, exchange little notes that read, 'Lunch with me tomorrow – we'll fix it then.'

Parkinson thought that the best way to deal with dysfunctional groups was to keep them small and bypass them when necessary. But when you are trying to implement some new initiative, you will usually be forced to deal with some people who are lukewarm, or downright resistant, to the project. Focusing solely on the supportive people is not enough; you have to address the other people's concerns too.

DEFINING IDEA

Entrepreneurs are simply those who understand that there is little difference between obstacle and opportunity and are able to turn both to their advantage.

NICCOLO MACHIAVELLI

One way of doing this is to examine the 'key stakeholders' in a project, meaning those individuals who are in a position to influence others about the project, and to analyse their attitudes. One can rank the stakeholders by the degree of influence they have, and then evaluate each individual's attitude in, say, five categories from 'strongly supportive' to 'strongly against'. The ranking tells you which individuals are the most important to address.

Next, you need to decide how to address each individual. You don't have to convert them all to a unanimous wild enthusiasm; all you need is to get sufficient co-operation across the group to keep the project going.

There are four common sources of resistance: territoriality, company politics, lack of skills, and personal difficulties. 'Territorial' people may be resisting because they think the project is going to reduce their own area of control, and can often be persuaded to change their attitude by offering them a leadership role in the part of the project that is most closely tied to their own patch. 'Internal politics' people may be fearful that the project will hamper their career, or even eliminate their job – and they may even be correct. In such cases, a good tactic is to admit the threat, if it is justified, while publicising the benefits to others. Often the resisters will see the way things are going, and become a little more co-operative. Others may resist because they lack the skills to understand the project, which can be overcome by providing helpful, non-threatening training so that they can participate usefully. Finally, some people may be resisting because they have trouble at home; this needs to be handled diplomatically, and where appropriate, the person can be given a reduced workload or compassionate leave.

This kind of stakeholder analysis may seem rather controlling and Machiavellian, and it is, but many organisations use the method and it works well. By obtaining a majority in support of the project and cutting the less enthusiastic people some slack, it's possible to achieve an organisational goal without stepping on too many toes as you go along.

HERE'S AN IDEA FOR YOU

To overcome someone who is resisting a project, the keys are good planning and identifying their reasons for resisting accurately. Almost always, a person resists because they are afraid that they are going to lose something; if you can work out what it is, you can offer something that compensates for it sufficiently for them to improve their attitude. Trampling all over them should be kept as a last resort.

30 BETTER BRAINSTORMING

A committee is organic rather than mechanical in its nature; it is not a structure but a plant.

Brainstorming is a well-known technique for generating ideas from a group, and there is a dynamic variation of it that can be used in large groups to obtain major gains in bureaucratic efficiency. By getting members of different departments, and of different organisations along the supply chain, all together in one room for a period of one to three days, solutions to problems of this kind can be found much more rapidly than in any other consultative process.

DEFINING IDEA

Creative thinking is not a talent, it is a skill that can be learnt. It empowers people by adding strength to their natural abilities which improves teamwork, productivity and where appropriate profits.

EDWARD DE BONO

GE, the US multinational, calls this technique a 'Work-Out' (meaning 'getting the unnecessary work out of the system'). As with any kind of group work, the key lies in carefully planning and orchestrating the event, and in implementing a determined follow-up process in the weeks after the event has been held. At the beginning of the event, specific goals are set for the group, such as 'How can we cut the time it takes to issue purchase orders by 30% by the end of June?', or 'How can we cut customer complaints by 80% within four months from now?' These targets must be measurable, realistic and have a clear deadline, but ideally should also challenge participants to stretch themselves and come up with original solutions to the problem.

Work-Outs start with an upbeat introduction that gives an overview of the problem and sets the goal, followed by warm-up exercises that show likely sources of difficulty. Then the group is split up into teams to brainstorm high-level ideas, after which the entire group meets to evaluate, pick and prioritise the ideas. The teams then work on the ideas to come up with detailed proposals that analyse the risk and suggest criteria for measuring progress. Finally, the teams present their proposals to a senior manager in front of the whole group for an immediate 'yes or no' decision – this is a key feature of the Work-Out, which prevents it from becoming just another talking shop and galvanises people into doing their best work.

The approved projects are assigned to 'owners', who are given the authority to push them through; often their regular work is temporarily reassigned to others in order to speed up the process. 'Owners' meet regularly with the senior managers to monitor progress, and are given teams, which may include people who did not attend the Work-Out, to implement the project. At a set date there is a final review where the success or failure of each project is assessed, and the results, good or bad, are communicated to all the participants and made available to the company at large.

HERE'S AN IDEA FOR YOU

When arranging a large-scale brainstorming event of this kind, make sure that you select the participants carefully for the value that they can contribute. For example, people who are known to be sceptical or cynical, but are well thought of by others, can make a very useful contribution, but most of the participants should be chosen either because they have relevant expertise, or because they will be able to implement any solution that comes up.

31 WHAT'S WRONG WITH CRONYISM?

Dr. Wu smiles enigmatically and points to the heap. 'None of them are any good', he says briefly.

It's annoying if you're not one of the cronies, of course, but what's wrong with cronyism really? Parkinson doesn't tell us – he's more concerned with making the point that other methods of choosing candidates for a position attract too many applicants. However, if pressed, he might have said that in general cronyism doesn't seem to produce worse results than other systems.

Cronyism is actually quite hard to define; after all, almost everyone relies on support networks of various kinds, and asks friends to do them favours. Should that be seen as cronyism, or just as having good interpersonal skills? Lots of business gets done through having good relationships, for example. In situations where trust is important, it is natural to rely on your friends.

Nevertheless, most of us feel that meritocracy must be a fairer system than cronyism. But if you look at an extreme example, such as Singapore, where the government stresses its fierce commitment to meritocracy, you find some obvious problems. In Singapore, meritocracy is quite narrowly defined as academic excellence, particularly in law and the sciences. Regardless of race, creed or colour, young Singaporeans who do well in higher education, preferably with a degree or two from a good British or American university, get fast-tracked into the upper echelons of Singaporean business and government. That might be fine, except no one else seems to get a look-in. If you haven't done well academically in one of a narrow and one-sided range of academic subjects, you just don't get to the top. Over the last few decades since independence, Singapore has developed into a stratified society in which the elite is largely composed of narrow-minded, prudish, risk-averse conformists. To the non-elite, the system looks just as rotten as the crony capitalism in neighbouring Malaysia.

Perhaps the answer is to confine anti-cronyism measures to the public sector alone, and leave business to sink or swim in whatever way it can. That's a commonly held sentiment in the US. But in the aftermath of the global financial crisis that begin in 2007 it has become clear that 'revolving door' cronyism (where senior executives moved through a 'revolving door' between top financial firms and government posts) played a role in loosening regulatory controls, which led directly to an insane lending spree and the sub-prime mortgage crisis. In this case, cronyism hurt everybody.

HERE'S AN IDEA FOR YOU

Perhaps the case against favouritism is most clear cut in parents' relationships with their children. While experts disagree about how harmful favouritism is in the long term, most accept that severe cases of favouritism indicate serious dysfunction. But it's impossible to be fair all the time, so how do you know if you are showing too much favouritism? Here are three questions to ask: Does each of your children feel he or she is your favourite? Do you try to give the same amount of attention to each child? Do you try not to compare your children in conversation? If you can answer 'yes' to all three, you're probably doing OK!

32 REFORMING REFORMS?

Politicians and taxpayers have assumed (with occasional phases of doubt) that a rising total in the number of civil servants must reflect a growing amount of work to be done.

In the UK, governments, whatever their political hue, are constantly reorganising the bureaucracy. Day in and day out, newspapers and radio programmes are filled with discussions of the pros and cons of various reforms that have happened, are about to happen, or ought to happen. We're generally told that these reforms will be beneficial in some way, but Parkinsonians naturally suspect that, however well-intentioned the reforms, they will be subject to Parkinson's Law.

DEFINING IDEA

Believing in progress does not mean believing that any progress has yet been made.

FRANZ KAFKA

According to a 2010 report by the National Audit Office (NAO), between 1980 and 2009, 25 new government departments were created, of which 13 have not survived. Two of them, the Department for Business, Enterprise and Regulatory Reform and the Department for Innovation, Universities and Skills, came and went in less than two years (2007–2009). Between 2005 and 2009, there were more than 90 reorganisations of government departments and agencies and, of these, 51 reorganisations were analysed by the report, whose total cost was £780 million.

In spite of all this activity and expenditure, the NAO found that many government bodies did not set reorganisation budgets or track the cost of making the changes. Parliament was unable to acquire information on reorganisation costs even when it did exist, because government departments are not required to divulge the information. Even in cases where the benefits of the reorganisation were primarily non-financial, central government departments did not measure the benefits that were intended to be achieved (these were often defined vaguely) and so could not assess whether they outweighed the costs, or indeed if the benefits had been achieved at all. In some cases, significant reorganisations were superseded within two years by a new and different reorganisation.

Another problem has been that most departments started reorganising without clear plans and had to make them up as they went along, according to the NAO. One of the reasons for this was that the reorganisations generally began as soon as they were announced, and that the reasons for the reorganisation were described so broadly that people didn't know why the reorganisation was necessary, or what benefits were to be achieved.

As Parkinson says, 'No one has been idle. All have done their best.' But it does make you wonder if the taxes we pay on our hard-earned money are really being spent quite as wisely as they could be. You couldn't make this stuff up. It might even be funny, if we weren't paying for it.

HERE'S AN IDEA FOR YOU

Were you made redundant in the latest government reorganisation? Perhaps all is not lost – maybe you can become a consultant. With your expertise, range of contacts and inside knowledge, you may be ideally placed to hire yourself back to your department for a healthy daily fee to help fix the cock-ups you knew were coming. And if you are good at what you do, you may be able to get a new job at a specialist management consultancy firm once you have exhausted the possibilities of obtaining work from your former employer on your own.

33 EFFICIENCY AT THE NHS

... this is a matter in which faith and doubt seem equally misplaced.

As one of the world's largest employers, soaking up almost 1.5 million of Britain's workforce, you might think that the NHS would be a prime target for Parkinson-style criticism. And, indeed, it is. But much of the criticism may be misplaced. For example, while the number of staff grew by 27.9% between 2000 and 2010, a staggering growth rate, was it really due to Parkinson's Law? In other words, was it the managers who were the main drivers of the expansion? Or was it driven by a political agenda external to the NHS, or by public demand for more healthcare, or by professional groups, such as doctors, or by other causes? And was the continuation of the NHS recruitment drive after the global financial crisis began in 2007 intended not to create further permanent expansion, but to 'fatten the pig' before the inevitable cuts, by creating a layer of expendable people who would be the first to go, as some have claimed? It is not at all clear that we can attribute the expansion to bureaucratic managers alone.

DEFINING IDEA

In the long-run every Government is the exact symbol of its People, with their wisdom and unwisdom; we have to say, Like People like Government.

THOMAS CARLYLE, HISTORIAN

What's more, a lot of the accusations that the NHS has a bloated bureaucracy seems to cherry-pick the evidence. Much has been made of the fact that the rate of increase in the number of managers between 2000 and 2011 (over 60%) exceeded the rate of increase in the number of doctors and nurses. But managers make up a tiny proportion of the NHS workforce: by 2010 they consisted of only about 3% of the entire staff. And, it is argued, more managers were needed to run all the new systems and rules that were imposed from the outside, from government policy, during the period. Parkinson wasn't against managers *per se* – they have their place in any organisation – and in the case of the NHS it doesn't seem to be true that a growth in the number of pen-pushers was the central problem.

There does seem to be some consensus that the NHS is not as efficient as it could be, but little agreement on where the inefficiencies lie. The top management consultancy firm McKinsey produced a report in 2010 suggesting that the NHS could cut 15–22% of its current budget by efficiency savings across a wide range of activities; the proposed savings included better drug purchasing methods, better scheduling of clinical rooms, and selling off empty buildings and land, none of which involved reducing the quality of medical care. Predictably, perhaps, no one liked the report, which was rejected by both the Labour and the Coalition governments, and was widely misrepresented until it was leaked. So the case of the NHS seems to show that Parkinson never discussed one of the most important sources of bureaucratic growth: politics and policy.

HERE'S AN IDEA FOR YOU

Cutting budgets causes pain because it involves effort and change, but it doesn't necessarily mean doing without. For example, do you withdraw cash on your credit card, or make five car trips to the shops every day? Making simple changes can often save a lot of money.

34 THRIFT

They would like to demonstrate, before the meeting ends, that they are alive to all that is going on.

In his chapter entitled 'High Finance', Parkinson satirises committee members who are incapable of understanding the details of major spending plans, but who spend huge amounts of time arguing about low-cost items in order to show that they are making a contribution. But, in the public sector, even this misplaced form of thrift seems to be absent.

DEFINING IDEA

An expert is a person who avoids small error as he sweeps on to the grand fallacy.

BENJAMIN STOLBERG, AUTHOR

Every so often, dynamic business tycoons are parachuted into government to find out why it is so inefficient. These captains of industry, so the thinking goes, clearly know how to run a tight ship in their own firms, so perhaps they will show us how to do it. In 2010 Sir Philip Green, the colourful boss of British Home Stores, was asked by the new Coalition government to review government spending. His report was polemical rather than objective, but produced some amusing headline-getters, mostly to do with a failure to buy centrally: prices paid for printing leaflets were many times the going rate; 98% of government mobile phone use was with one provider, yet it had 68 different contracts on different terms with that provider; prices for staff vending machine products varied by 38%; IT contractors were charging daily rates of £1000 per individual; breaks in leasing contracts for buildings were not exploited, resulting in millions of pounds of unnecessary rent payments.

Actually, if those were the worst examples of waste that Sir Philip Green could find, the government isn't doing too badly. And his main recommendation, to centralise purchasing and cost monitoring, might work well in a private business, but you can see how Parkinson's Law might make that a very poor solution to the problem in government. The report complained that accurate data on expenditure was often unavailable (one wonders whether people just didn't want to give it to him) and stated in the introduction, 'I am deliberately not going to place a total number on the waste and/or the saving'. That's quite a contrast to the careful, thorough work contained in efficiency-saving reports like McKinsey's on the NHS discussed in Chapter 33.

There are trade-offs in efficiency measures in any organisation. Suppose, for instance, you want to reduce the time staff spend not working at their desks, so you decide to introduce a strict rota system for going to the loo, at prescribed times. Even if you could implement such a system – which you could, in a dictatorship – would it really be the most sensible way to cut down time-wasting? Sir Philip was probably right that central purchasing would save money, but his sloppily prepared, ill-considered report doesn't go into any real detail on how that might be achieved in a civil service context. All the Sir Humphreys in central government must have had a good laugh at his expense on this occasion.

HERE'S AN IDEA FOR YOU

Cutting costs is a real art and it's possible to make bad mistakes that have very serious consequences. After a Texas oil refinery owned by BP exploded in 2005, killing 15 people, government investigators found that earlier cost-cutting had played a major role. That error cost BP a fine of $50 million and compensation of $1.6 billion.

35 THE MYTH OF TALENT

... the writing of Greek verse might prove to be the sole accomplishment that some candidates had or ever would have.

Parkinson satirised the civil service examination system of the late 19th and early 20th centuries for testing candidates in their knowledge of ancient Latin and Greek rather than in something useful. Today, it's easy for us to feel that our modern meritocratic society has abolished such absurdities. Contemporary methods of choosing the talented people who are likely to rise to the very top are far more effective than the amateurish, class-based techniques of the past.

DEFINING IDEA

What mankind wants is not talent; it is purpose.
EDWARD BULWER-LYTTON,
POLITICIAN AND NOVELIST

When a major management consultancy conducted an in-depth study of this a few years ago in the US, it decided that what really made the top firms stand out from the rest was that they nurtured top management 'talent' and paid them very high salaries; this finding gave force to a general trend in big business to create an elite echelon of leaders by finding the best people and drowning them in money.

Increasingly, however, people are beginning to wonder if the systems that human resources departments use to identify and develop future high flyers are really picking the right people. According the *Wall Street Journal*, the average pay of CEOs in the US is now hundreds of times higher than that of their average employees. Chris Bones, of Henley Business School, argues that the talent myth has created a 'L'Oreal generation' of top executives (L'Oreal promotes its cosmetics with the catchphrase, 'Because you're worth it') who aren't particularly effective. A number of studies have found no correlation between salary and performance among top executives. Other studies find that a high IQ (a key criterion used in identifying high flyers) has only a low correlation with job performance. Psychologists looking at the personalities of top leaders suggest that the talent system fails to filter out people with personality flaws that lead them to make disastrous mistakes once they are running a company. And a torrent of recent books and articles attacks the whole concept of cultivating leadership, arguing that most of the assumptions used are baseless.

It seems clear that current methods of identifying and nurturing future leaders within large organisations are far from perfect. The 2001 collapse of the energy giant Enron, for instance, was directly due to the lunatic actions of 'L'Oreal generation' high flyers. It was the super-smart, hothoused geniuses in the investing banking industry who led the charge into crazy risks that resulted in the global financial crisis. So, while we may laugh at the idea that Greek and Latin scholars make the best leaders, we shouldn't feel too smug about today's system of picking them either.

HERE'S AN IDEA FOR YOU

It's now widely accepted by psychologists that the number of sociopaths is disproportionately high at the top of most professions. Such people can do you a lot of harm, yet they're hard to spot, so how can you protect yourself? One way is to have a 'three strikes and you're out' rule: sociopaths are often shameless deceivers, so if you suspect that someone has tricked you more than once, the next time they do it, put some permanent distance between you.

36 LYING TO GET A JOB

On occasion a successful applicant may have been impersonated at the examination by someone else, subsequently proving unable to write Greek verse when the occasion arose.

When Cardinal Richelieu, the 17th century statesman, was 21 years old he went to Rome to be ordained as a bishop, although he was four years under the minimum age. On being informed that the young man had committed perjury to become bishop, the Pope is reported to have laughed, 'this fellow will either be a great knave or a great man.'

DEFINING IDEA

Half the world knows not how the other half lies.

GEORGE HERBERT, POET

Judging by the long-standing precautions taken by Britain's oldest universities, a lot of people were paying others to take their exams for them in the 19th century. And the introduction of civil service exams by the Victorians was, in part, because some people with university degrees were proving to be unsatisfactory. These days, the battery of exams and vetting procedures for the top entry-level jobs used by the civil service and most major corporations seem to do a good job at picking the candidates who have the 'competencies' that the particular organisation wants.

Nevertheless, there are claims that an increasing number of job applicants are misrepresenting or embellishing their records. One survey of the financial sector found that in 2010 the number of applicants concealing a criminal conviction was 3%, treble the rate of the previous year. Other researchers claim that more than three quarters of all CVs are embellished, and a quarter are actually fraudulent. Unsurprisingly, most of these surveys are produced by firms that offer background check services, so one might legitimately wonder if they are biased. It's not clear that CV fraud is really a serious problem. Although nobody wants unqualified pilots or doctors, for instance, they are not that hard to detect at the application stage. And as for embellishment, the corporate cultures in many firms seem to expect it – presenting your skills and experience in the best possible light is supposed to be a virtue, after all, as it demonstrates your enthusiasm, selling ability and 'people skills'.

The Richelieu phenomenon hasn't disappeared either; in 2011 the colourful German defence minister, Baron Karl-Theodor zu Guttenberg, had to resign after a law professor discovered that the Baron had plagiarised parts of his doctoral thesis, which was subsequently revoked by the University of Bayreuth. 'Baron Cut-and-Paste' was a popular figure who had enjoyed a meteoric career before the scandal. He was defended vigorously by the German Chancellor, Angela Merkel, who argued, not unreasonably, that she wanted him as a minister, not an academic assistant. But in these democratic times, Merkel can't just laugh off the problem the way the Pope did back in 1607.

HERE'S AN IDEA FOR YOU

The line between presenting yourself well and misrepresentation isn't always easy to draw. For example, we're told that everything on a CV should be relevant to the job you are applying for – which gives you permission to be selective about your past duties. And saying how much you adored working at a company that you really despised is expected; if you don't, you might be perceived as having a bad attitude. The bottom line is to use your common sense, and be ready to back up every statement you make.

37 MANAGEMENT VOODOO

He will pause, sniff, and nod wisely, and it should be obvious at once that he *knows*.

There are so many management gurus these days, and they come in so many different varieties, that it's hard to know which ones to take seriously. They range from the long-established names, like Peter Drucker, W. Edwards Deming and Tom Peters, to New Age mystics like Deepak Chopra and self-help giants like Anthony Robbins. Maybe they all have something useful to say, although one wonders who gets much out of books that claim to know how to apply the leadership methods of Attila the Hun, Aristotle, or characters from Star Trek. But given that a lot of management theorising is so astoundingly boring, maybe the books with wacky titles do manage to get some basic insights through to their readership.

DEFINING IDEA

I have been saying for many years that we are using the word 'guru' only because 'charlatan' is too long to fit into a headline.
PETER DRUCKER

Part of the problem is in distinguishing management ideas that are meaningful in the long term from ones that merely address a current problem, or flatter a special interest group. Lucy Kellaway, a *Financial Times* journalist who runs a one-woman crusade against management drivel, complained recently that a Women's Conference in California, intended to empower women in the workplace, consisted mainly of meaningless self-help affirmations like 'being who we are is in fact the greatest gift that we can give ourselves'. Lucy Kellaway's view is that women may now be catching up with men in their ability to talk management 'guff'.

Perhaps we should leave aside the non-academic management gurus, and focus on the research being done in universities and business schools that, one hopes, have higher standards of rigour. But even in the dreaming spires of academe all is not as it should be, according to Josep Rosanas, an accounting professor at the IESE business school in Spain. Rosanas thinks that scholars 'often behave as if there were a widely accepted paradigm and that we only had to discuss minor points' of management theory, when in fact there are major problems. According to Rosanas, these include: overspecialisation, which prevents experts from solving simple problems in other areas of business; incentives to 'pseudo-inquiry', where people try to prove a preconceived idea or simply argue for a proposition without caring if it is true or not; a tendency to misapply concepts taken from economics, such as the idea that all people seek to maximise their selfish goals in a rational way; and a huge pressure on academics to publish new articles and books, which damages their quality. As Parkinson might have pointed out, academics themselves are not immune to the inexorable workings of Parkinson's Law.

HERE'S AN IDEA FOR YOU

Don't just assume that because some management guru's theory is being touted as the holy writ that it is any good: investigate! What evidence does it offer that it can work, has ever worked, or might work in your organisation? A long series of two-paragraph case studies proves nothing — they're just anecdotes, and there may have been bias in their selection. And can you even tell what principles the theory is using? Insist on thinking critically about these propositions, and encourage your colleagues to do the same.

38 NEPOTISM

In the event of the candidate's saying, 'Well, my father is a fishmonger in Cheapside,' the interview was virtually over.

Even in these democratic times when organisations need to be more efficient, and to draw upon a much wider range of candidates than ever before, the interrelated phenomena of cronyism, nepotism, and the development of elites have not disappeared. Nepotism, in particular, seems to occur in intensely competitive situations where the stakes are very high indeed. In the intense and bloody power struggles of Renaissance Italy, for example, it's easy to see why noble families like the Borgias and the Medicis had to use nepotism to survive.

DEFINING IDEA

Many a live wire would be a dead one except for his connections.

W. MIZNER, PLAYWRIGHT

It's striking that even in the 21st century we see examples of nepotism at the top all over the world, across every political system. For example, the Middle East is famous for its nepotistic dynasties, from Saudi Arabia to Libya, but you also see political dynasties in western democracies, such as the Kennedy and the Bush families in the US, and the Benns and the Salisburys in the UK. In Hollywood, there are many examples of movie dynasties, such as the Sheens, the Coppolas and the Fondas. In big business, there are the Murdochs, the Trumps and the Fords. And often, you can't see the family connections because the surnames are different. But even family dynasties tend not to last very long – after two or three generations, the bonds of nepotism tend to break down in the face of competition from others.

According to Adam Bellow, son of the famous novelist Saul Bellow, nepotism isn't necessarily all bad. Bellow argues that for the poor immigrants pouring into the Americas during the 19th and early 20th centuries, nepotism was a means of survival. The US was built by immigrants who stuck together in ethnic groups and financed their family-owned businesses through their extended family networks. It wasn't until the Depression of the 1930s, says Bellow, that nepotism became discredited and these firms began to change their character as American business became professionalised.

Nepotism, then, is a natural response to certain kinds of challenging conditions. In organisations that need to choose the best people for the job, nepotism can only be tolerated if the beneficiaries are actually very good at what they do. Having a powerful relative may give you a head start, but if you can't deliver the goods, other people will overtake you. Nepotism is a strategy in competitive games, but it is not necessarily the winning strategy, especially not in the long term.

HERE'S AN IDEA FOR YOU

Is nepotism really preventing you from rising in your organisation? In most public sector organisations it really isn't a major factor, and although some major commercial firms are controlled by families, they can still be great places to work and offer attractive career opportunities. Don't confuse nepotism with other, more insidious forms of discrimination, like cronyism, which can trip you up if you aren't alert to what is going on. In fact, nepotists may actually treat you more fairly, because they need allies with real ability – in the end, identifying what you have to offer, and who needs your skills and abilities, is the best strategy to deal with these perennial problems.

39 SKUNK WORKS

We cannot compete with Toprank. Here in Lowgrade we do useful work, meeting the needs of the country. Let us be content with that.

DEFINING IDEA

'General, I believe in the well-known golden rule. If you've got the gold, you make the rules.'

BEN RICH, SKUNK WORKS

Management theorists like to generalise from particular cases. If Company Y is fantastically successful and well-run, theorists want to identify its secret recipe and show how other companies can do the same. The trouble is, successful companies are often unique, and therefore very hard to imitate.

One such organisation is Skunk Works, a small semi-autonomous unit within Lockheed that between the 1940s and the 1980s designed a series of military aircraft for the US military, such as the U2 spy plane and the first stealth aircraft, that revolutionised aviation and gave the US a substantial lead in the Cold War arms race. Under the inspired leadership of two bosses, Kelly Johnson and, later, Ben Rich, Skunk Works became legendary for its ability to navigate its way through the bureaucratic labyrinth of the defence establishment to produce outstandingly innovative machines on time and on budget.

As part of a commercial firm, Skunk Works had to make a profit, bidding competitively against other firms to win government contracts for each new project, and finding ways to cope with the massively inefficient bureaucracy of the US government. What made matters worse was the very high levels of secrecy involved, which created huge layers of extra cost that were very hard to predict or control. For example, in 1964, President Lyndon Johnson announced the existence of a new aircraft, the RS-71, but in a slip of the tongue called it the 'SR-71'; the Air Force then insisted that Skunk Works change the name to SR-71 on 29,000 blueprints and drawings, costing a fortune.

For much of its life Skunk Works operated out of a two-storey hangar at an airport in Burbank California, and employed only a few hundred people, yet it generated a huge revenue for its company: $6 billion on the first stealth fighters alone. Its reputation as an innovative, streamlined and anti-bureaucratic operation has encouraged managers in other organisations to try to imitate its methods, with limited success. Now that much of the Skunk Works story has been declassified, however, it is clear that the unit was often not that efficient. For example, at one point it was forced to accept an efficiency team imposed on it by the Air Force to find ways to prevent 'foreign object damage', caused when careless workers left stray objects inside engines. 'You'll thank me for it later,' an air force general told Ben Rich, who later admitted that he was right.

The real reasons for the success of Skunk Works? A combination of determination, flexibility, integrity, brilliance and risk-taking in a market that had very strong demand and only a few competitors. And that's not a combination that can be applied easily to many businesses.

HERE'S AN IDEA FOR YOU

On several occasions Skunk Works incurred major losses by cancelling projects and returning millions of dollars to the government. Although this was painful in the short term, it generated enormous goodwill with its main customer, the US military, and created an invaluable atmosphere of trust. Treat your customers well, and they'll come back.

40 BUSINESS TRAVEL

Nowadays the technique is to lay before the great man the programme of a conference at Helsinki in June, a congress in Adelaide in July, and a convention in Ottawa in August, each lasting about three weeks.

DEFINING IDEA

Travel is only glamorous in retrospect.

PAUL THEROUX

Parkinson suggested that a good way of persuading senior figures in an organisation to retire was to devise an exhausting series of trips for them around the world. From anecdotal evidence, this is a technique that is still used. One manager of my acquaintance tells the story of how he became irritated by a colleague who constantly accused him of going off on 'jollies' (he flew 100 days a year) when in fact the experience was so gruelling that you had to be super-fit just to stay sane. Eventually the manager got his opportunity for payback: the colleague was going to a conference in the US, and the manager suggested that he go on to the Far East to meet with several large clients in different locations. The colleague eagerly agreed, and a fiendish two month trip was devised for him that exploited all the tiresome aspects of Asia: the four hour trips from downtown Jakarta to the airport, the obligatory all night drinking sessions with clients, the airlines that only let you carry ridiculously small hand luggage, the absence of aspirin, the endless visa problems and so on. The real coup was to arrange weekly flights to the Arabian

Gulf, where the hapless colleague had to wait through the night in the stifling heat for connecting flights back to sub-zero temperatures in Korea and northern China. Five weeks into the trip, the colleague threw in the towel and came home on sick leave. He never talked about 'jollies' again.

The growth of business travel seems to be subject to Parkinson's Law; one recent survey found that more than half of European business travellers think that their trips are unnecessary. Italians travel the most frequently (19% of respondents travelled more than once a month) and reported suffering the most stress from travel. More than 60% of Germans, Italians and Dutch thought that their trips were needless, with the Swedes scoring a low 35%. Other studies suggest that many businesses allow their employees to arrange their business travel themselves, wasting an estimated £1.5 billion in the UK alone in lost discounts and high-cost managerial time. A centralised system of travel buying is desirable, according to some experts, especially in light of the drive to reduce companies' carbon footprints – although others are complaining that the carbon reduction movement is creating whole new layers of useless bureaucracy.

HERE'S AN IDEA FOR YOU

There is something slightly unsavoury about the frequent flyer promotional schemes run by airlines. Many companies allow employees to build up flyer miles in their own names, in effect giving them some free personal travel. Some countries tax this as a personal benefit, while civil servants in other countries, notably Australia, are strictly forbidden to use frequent flyer miles, even to upgrade to a better class on a legitimate business trip. Increasingly, frequent flyers are complaining that they find it difficult to acquire tickets with frequent flyer points, and that some schemes give ridiculously few points for long haul travel. All in all, it's a distraction that most people could easily give up.

41 WHEN AN ENTIRE COUNTRY COOKS THE BOOKS

Third-rateness has become a principle of policy.

In May 2010 the government of Greece obtained a $146 billion bailout agreement from the EU and the IMF in order to service its massive debts. There were fears that the country's near-insolvency could spread to other countries in the eurozone and lead to a collapse of the euro as a currency. The European Commission's economy commissioner, Olli Rehn, remarked that 'Greece is indeed a unique and particular case in the EU. Greece has had particularly precarious debt dynamics and Greece is the only member state that cheated with its statistics for years and years.'

DEFINING IDEA

Corruption has never been compulsory.

ANTHONY EDEN, BRITISH PRIME MINISTER

That's an extraordinarily strong statement for a normally tight-lipped EU bureaucrat to make, and indicates the extent of the worries over the euro's future. In order to work, the common currency depends upon the willingness of member states within the eurozone to provide a regular stream of economic and fiscal data to ensure that they are working within the monetary and budgetary rules, without which confidence in the currency would evaporate.

Eurostat, the European Commission's office of statistics, published a damning report in 2010 that gave details of consistent misreporting of figures by Greece stretching back many years, and stating that errors in the figures for 2007, 2008, and 2009 were 'deliberate'. Over the years Eurostat officials had repeatedly gone to Greece to investigate the problems and to agree upon improving procedures. Eurostat had received many assurances that the problems would be rectified but nothing had been done.

The 2010 bailout gave the EU and the IMF the opportunity to impose reforms on the failing country. Many of these 'austerity' measures were simply common sense. Greece's chaotic retirement and pension system was heading for collapse, not only because of its generous deals to many special interest groups, but more importantly because employers were not paying employers' contributions to the pension schemes. Tax evasion was endemic and there were large arrears. In the public sector, which had grown rapidly between 2000 and 2008, many institutions were running huge deficits, including hospitals, which had deliberately understated their debts by 1 billion euros between 2005 and 2008, according to Eurostat.

With the introduction of the reforms, violent mass protests and strikes occurred during 2010 and 2011, as had been predicted by many observers. Interestingly, public fury was directed not so much at preventing the cuts, than at oligarchs in political parties and state institutions that, it is claimed, had connived at the development of a system of government that could only be sustained by cheating its partner states in the EU. Greece's woes illustrate just how bad things can get when injelitance in the bureaucracy becomes a matter of policy.

HERE'S AN IDEA FOR YOU

In the years leading up to the crisis, most economic reports on Greece were positive, and the problems discussed above were presented as getting better, when in fact they were getting worse. Normally we expect government sources to be the most reliable providers of statistics, but it's worth remembering that they are not always reliable. Healthy scepticism is not 'negativity', as some people seem to think – it is an essential defence against being misled!

42 TRANSPARENCY

The stalwarts will carefully avoid mentioning the main subject of the debate.

'Transparency' is the watchword of our age; everywhere you look, organisations are trying to make themselves more transparent, or explaining why they can't. New international NGOs have sprung up to promote the concept, like Transparency International in Berlin (which is 'leading the fight against corruption') and the Global Transparency Initiative (which, hilariously, currently provides no information about itself on its website under the heading 'About the GTI').

DEFINING IDEA

Sunlight is the best disinfectant.

WILLIAM O DOUGLAS, US SUPREME COURT JUDGE

Parkinson makes no mention of the principle of transparency in his book; it's a new development since his day. For those of us who are outside bureaucracies, transparency looks like a good thing – we often want to know things that the bureaucrats won't tell us. Transparency is claimed to be a key element in promoting greater democracy, and is closely associated with another buzz phrase, 'civil society'. This refers to non-governmental organisations such as charities, advocacy groups, trade unions and community organisations, which are supposed to play a positive role in encouraging citizens to participate more fully in the democratic process. Some of these organisations are becoming very powerful bureaucracies in their own right, so it is perhaps ironic that many of them are run by people who have not been elected – but that's another story.

Bureaucrats tend naturally to hoard information, so it seems sensible to try to encourage bureaucracies to cut down on their treasure trove of secrets. But, as many people have pointed out, this is an uphill struggle, and possibly unwinnable. Take the IMF, for example – as an important global institution that bails out countries when they are going broke, you might think that it would welcome demands for more openness. But according to a 2008 report by the Global Transparency Initiative, the IMF did not recognise the right of access to information, had no firm rules on what information could be kept secret, did not 'have a strong or visible stance on promoting its freedom of information', and provided inadequate protection for whistleblowers. Numerous documents produced by the IMF over recent years, on the other hand, claim that great strides are being made in creating better transparency within the organisation, and indeed it now has an 'integrity hotline' that people can use to report allegations of 'misconduct' (which is hardly the same thing as promoting transparency). Nor does the IMF's amended transparency policy (effective March 17, 2010) fill the outside observer with confidence; it's an 11-page document written in impenetrable legalese that is really a masterpiece of opacity. As the GTI's report says, while the GTI 'strongly believes in the right to information, it also recognizes that implementation of such a regime at the IMF presents political problems'. Exactly so, but you could say the same of the whole transparency/civil society movement. And the IMF governors are unelected appointees, nicely insulated from the horrible mass of voters.

HERE'S AN IDEA FOR YOU

One of the more promising developments in the drive for transparency is the emergence of independent whistleblowing sites on the internet. They're a mixed bag, of course, and have provoked enormous controversy but some of them (such as Wikileaks) have published accurate information that governments didn't want us to know. So make use of them and defend them, or else they'll quietly get shut down.

43 CENTRALISED PLANNING

Examples abound of new institutions coming into existence with a full establishment of deputy directors, consultants and executives … And experience proves that such an institution will die.

Parkinson believed that top-down planning often did not work, but it's hard to see how developing nations can avoid it. With their growing populations, they are under pressure to adopt modernisation wholesale as quickly as possible, and benefit from the systems and technologies that have been developed elsewhere. And sometimes it has worked well; Mexico's economy, for instance, was transformed during the 1890s by the rapid building of a railway system that was entirely a result of 'top-down' planning by the clique surrounding the dictator of the time, Porfirio Diaz, who was subsequently overthrown in the Mexican Revolution.

DEFINING IDEA

If you want to make God laugh, show him your plans.
WOODY ALLEN

Nevertheless, there are indeed plenty of examples of such programmes ending badly, as Parkinson points out. What's more, these examples cover the entire political spectrum, from communist regimes to right-wing dictatorships, and a wide range of economic theories. For instance, in the 1960s and 1970s many countries were encouraged to try to develop an industrial base as a method of 'import substitution', but without having any hope of achieving the necessary economies of scale. This resulted in lunatic schemes such as Peru's car manufacturing industry, which was unable to make cars cheaper than they could be imported, and in any case had almost no potential customers, since very few Peruvians could afford to buy a car of any kind.

For the governments of developing countries, the problems can be a very complex balancing act. Economic success may help a regime to stay in power, but this may depend upon grabbing short-lived opportunities to try to make them work. This happened in oil-rich Algeria after the world price hikes in oil of 1973 and 1974 enabled the then president, Houari Boumediene, to double state investment in infrastructure and heavy industry. Steel mills, power plants and tractor factories appeared almost overnight, but when the president died in 1978 the policy of rapid industrialisation was reversed, in favour of decentralisation and privatisation, which increased the already perilously high operating costs of the new industries. A civil war in the mid-1990s destroyed many of the factories.

Although high oil prices have once again come to Algeria's rescue, the state has not distributed much of its wealth, and unemployment and poverty remain high. The top-down, centralised industrialised planning of the 1970s could have worked and led to a diversified economy less dangerously dependent on oil. It's a salutary reminder that economic planning without political stability is a recipe for disaster.

HERE'S AN IDEA FOR YOU

If you are undertaking a major project, don't get carried away by your optimism. Do a proper risk analysis, consider how things might go wrong, and face up to the possibility of a worst-case scenario. Then, make detailed contingency plans of how you would deal with every one of the possible problems you have identified in your risk analysis, and don't be afraid to spend money on putting protection into place. Once the project is underway, don't forget to review your risk assessment regularly, and update your contingency plans as new issues arise.

44 THE BENEFITS LABYRINTH

There will soon be an actual competition is stupidity, people pretending to be even more brainless than they are.

Whatever your political views on the value of the UK's benefit system, it's pretty hard to argue that it can't be made more efficient. Granted, there have been periods in the past when the system was even more dysfunctional than it is today, but despite the improvements there are still some very big problems. The central issue is that it is incredibly complicated, which makes it almost impossible for many claimants to figure out what they are entitled to, and puts off some needy claimants from applying at all. Because the system is so complex, it is not transparent, which makes it very hard for governments to reform it, or for voters to understand what is really going on. The benefits system takes up about a quarter of total government spending and absorbs an enormous amount of claimants' (and bureaucrats') time, which might be usefully spent on more productive activities. The weird rules, and the constant threat of losing your entitlements, contributes to the 'poverty trap', where some claimants don't want to risk trying to get into work for fear of losing their benefits too soon.

DEFINING IDEA

There is hope, but not for us.

FRANZ KAFKA

Much could be done to improve the system without in any way reducing the amount of cash that claimants receive. Currently there are more than fifty benefits available, administered by several different authorities, including the Department of Work and Pensions, the Inland Revenue, the Department for Children, Schools and Families, the Department of Health, and local authorities. Because the rules for particular benefits overlap, it is very difficult to work out entitlements, and sometimes claimants have to apply for benefits to which they know they are not entitled, and will be refused, in order to gain access to a different benefit. The departments concerned have vast manuals, containing thousands of pages, to help them figure out how to apply the rules. Rules on such matters as how income is calculated, how part-time work is defined, and whether one benefit takes precedence over another, vary substantially between the different benefits. The number of forms that claimants have to fill in is staggering, and continues to grow, and the long delays before different departments come to different decisions about the same information provided by a claimant causes a lot of distress to a lot of people.

So what can be done about this Kafkaesque nightmare? One thing is to decide once and for all to stop endlessly tinkering with it – the rules have been constantly changing since the welfare system was first set up, and this is a major factor causing the system's over-complexity. Another would be to create a unified, simplified system run by a single lean, efficient department. But this could only happen if the major political parties could agree on a permanent set of efficient reforms; so far, this has not happened.

HERE'S AN IDEA FOR YOU

Breaking out of the benefits trap can be very hard indeed, but people who have been made redundant for the first time often do not realise this. If you suddenly find yourself out of work, don't put your energies into trying to get benefits – put them into getting another job.

45 IT COULD HAPPEN HERE

A diseased institution cannot reform itself.

Impersonality is characteristic of most bureaucracies, and is one of the features that allows bureaucrats to treat others inhumanely. According to some eminent psychologists, the highly developed bureaucracies of oppressive regimes, such as Nazi Germany, play a major role in persuading perfectly normal people to commit, or to facilitate, terrible crimes against humanity. This is done by creating a situation that demands bureaucratic obedience and takes away all personal responsibility for the actions – they are done in the name of the state.

DEFINING IDEA

Obedience is due only to legitimate powers.
JEAN JACQUES ROUSSEAU.
PHILOSOPHER

It's easy to label such toxic bureaucracies as aberrations, but there is evidence to the contrary, notably two famous sets of experiments carried out at Stanford University: the Milgram experiment on obedience to authority figures, in 1963, and the Stanford Prison Experiment, in which volunteers were randomly selected to play either guards or prisoners in a mock prison, in 1971. These experiments appear to demonstrate how easy it is to persuade normal people to do appalling things within an institutional context. The Milgram experiment fooled subjects into believing that they were administering real electric shocks to a 'learner' (played by an actor) whenever he got a question wrong, while the prison experiment had to be stopped after six days because the guards were becoming increasingly sadistic and prisoners were having breakdowns.

The experiments could not be repeated today because of much tighter ethical rules on experimentation.

More recently, Professor Philip Zimbardo, who conducted the 1971 Stanford Prison Experiment, gave expert evidence in the defence of a US army sergeant court-martialled for his role in the Abu Ghraib prison scandal in Iraq. According to Zimbardo, the Abu Ghraib guards would not have committed their horrendous crimes had it not been for the political, legal and economic forces that had created a situation which brought out the worst in them. He isn't merely blaming it all on the system – he believes that the human mind has 'an infinite capacity to make any one of us kind or cruel'.

We may not like to admit it, but cases of institutional abuse crop up everywhere, and frequently; we can't just pretend that it only ever happened in Stalinist Russia or Nazi Germany. For example, think of the many scandals that have occurred in children's institutions and old people's homes in civilised countries all over the world. If the system encourages it, or even is just indifferent to it, bad things start to happen in forgotten corners of the bureaucracy. Sometimes it is just petty meanness and dishonesty, but sometimes it gets a lot worse. This is one reason why transparency and accountability matter so much, and why we need whistleblowers and critics of the system: otherwise, sometimes, bureaucrats can become very dangerous indeed.

HERE'S AN IDEA FOR YOU

Zimbardo thinks we should cultivate individual 'heroism' as a counter to institutional pressures to do bad things, and has proposed 20 hints on how to do this. Here are three of them: never get cut off emotionally from your family and friends; be willing to admit your mistakes and cut your losses; and don't think you could never be influenced negatively by others, but recognise that you, too, are vulnerable.

46 RECRUITMENT HELL

Only a little thought is needed to convince us that the perfect advertisement would attract only one reply and that from the right man.

Parkinson was joking when he suggested that the ideal ad would attract only one applicant, but he was certainly correct in suggesting that putting more thought into designing the job specification is likely to attract the most appropriate candidates.

DEFINING IDEA

If you pick the right people and give them the opportunity to spread their wings – and put compensation as a carrier behind it – you almost don't have to manage them.
JACK WELCH. FORMER CEO OF GE

The best companies have excellent recruitment practices that are intended not only to capture high-quality employees, but also to promote a positive image of the firm to unsuccessful applicants, and to make the process as efficient as possible. Part or all of the process can be outsourced. For example, a well-designed pre-screening that involves a formalised telephone interview can be outsourced to a specialist recruitment service that can be relied on to execute the task properly. Most of the best firms prefer not to outsource the entire process, especially for executive positions. However, with the massive growth in recruitment agencies over the last few years, there is evidence that many firms are not using recruitment outsourcing intelligently.

According to a 2007 survey by Reed Consulting, many employers are not managing their recruitment carefully. For instance, 66% of job applicants received no response at all to their applications, according to Reed, which creates ill-will. Other common problems include not giving any feedback to unsuccessful applicants, providing insufficient information about the job and the organisation, and long delays during the recruitment process. Applicants complained a lot about being put on hold for a long period when telephoning the firm, and were particularly negative towards automated voice recognition systems that require them to answer a set of pre-recorded questions as part of the pre-screening process.

Further down the business food chain, it is clear that there are many firms that are appallingly sloppy when it comes to recruitment, failing to produce clear job specifications, skipping the pre-screening process, mismanaging online recruiting websites, failing to instruct recruitment agencies clearly, allowing second-rate agencies to inundate them with completely inappropriate candidates and CVs from current employees, and picking agencies solely on the basis of low commissions.

Recruitment is an expensive process when done properly, if you factor in the time it takes to plan and conduct it. Outsourcing part of the work is supposed to save the company money, but often many firms seem to be throwing the baby out with the bathwater by failing to manage the outsourcing process properly. Bad outsourcing practices lead to massive inefficiencies, bad PR, and bad hiring decisions; Parkinson could have written a whole new book about the lamentable state of current recruitment practices.

HERE'S AN IDEA FOR YOU

Here are some classic recruiting mistakes to avoid. Talking too much in the interview – the candidate should do most of the talking! Asking leading questions, like 'We love our customers here. Do you love your customers?' – what's the candidate going to say, 'No'? Failing to check the candidate's existing remuneration package – if you don't know what they are getting, how are you going to make them a better offer?

47 BAD LANGUAGE

Those who are too stupid to follow the proceedings. These are readily distinguishable by their tendency to mutter to each other: 'What is the fellow talking about?'

Language is dynamic, not fixed in stone. It is always changing, with new words being invented, and the meanings of old words changing. Much of this process is entirely natural, but there are plenty of individuals and organisations who try to alter language in their own interests. There are also bureaucracies dedicated to preventing the process, such as the Académie française, which has fought a long but losing battle against changes to the French language, such as the importation of English loan-words. In other countries, state-backed language academies are dedicated to changing the local language, such as in Turkey, where the Turkish Language Association does its best to invent new words to replace centuries-old Turkish words derived from Arabic and Persian.

DEFINING IDEA

If thought corrupts language, language can also corrupt thought.
GEORGE ORWELL

English has become the dominant language in international business, politics and science, and we tend to celebrate its extraordinary diversity, regarding objections to language change as fogeyish. But when the new language has a political agenda, or aims to deceive in order to gain a business objective, perhaps we should take more notice.

It takes a lot for a senior British civil servant to use bad language, so people sat up in surprise when in 2007 Sir Ivor Roberts, the ambassador to Rome, complained that in the Foreign Office, 'change-management agenda is written in Wall Street management speak already ... discredited by the time it is introduced. Synergies, best practice, benchmarking ... roll out, stakeholder ... fit for purpose, are all prime candidates for a game of bullshit bingo, a substitute for clarity and succinctness.' This is an interesting case of politicians using management speak in order to effect a 'Cultural Revolution', as Sir Ivor put it, within its own bureaucracy.

An alliance between arch-manipulators of language in politics and business is quite a scary combination. It brings us closer to the tyranny of 'newspeak' described in George Orwell's dystopian novel, *Nineteen Eighty-Four*. In the book, 'newspeak' is an artificially changed version of English (known as 'oldspeak') which has been purged of all words that might lead to political unorthodoxy, and is deliberately dumbed down and filled with euphemisms such as 'joycamp' for 'forced labour camp'. The aim of newspeak, according to the book, is to make 'all other modes of thought impossible'.

So does this mean we are heading for the kind of collectivist nightmare described by Orwell? Such a thing may have a lot of appeal to the bureaucratic mind. But given that so many other groups, from international NGOs to single-issue pressure groups, are successfully changing the language in other ways for conflicting ends, perhaps we have nothing to worry about.

HERE'S AN IDEA FOR YOU

Commercial and state bureaucracies inundate us with loaded language and weasel words that are designed to lead us in a certain direction, or to disguise what is going on. We can probably see through phrases like 'part of a nutritious breakfast' (which could apply to anything that was not actually poisonous) but what about 'hard-working families', much used by politicians of every hue, which makes listeners think it must apply to their own family, but could mean anything?

48 CUTTING THROUGH BUREAUCRACY

It is absurd the way these people at Much-Striving talk of their work, just as if they were in the Toprank class.

DEFINING IDEA

Energy and persistence conquer all things.

BENJAMIN FRANKLIN

The discovery of new medicines has long been thought to be the preserve of the giant, bureaucratic pharmaceutical companies, because only they have the resources needed to plough through endless blind alleys in research to find a handful of promising substances, and then to conduct large-scale tests, often involving tens of thousands of people, in order to obtain the approval of the notoriously strict Food and Drug Administration (FDA) in the US – the chief market, in terms of profits, for most new drugs.

On occasion, however, it has been possible to break this barrier. In 1973 two researchers, Herb Boyer and Stanley Cohen, found a way to transplant genes from a strand of DNA in a toad into bacteria. This breakthrough was the foundation of genetic engineering. In 1975 a young entrepreneur, Bob Swanson, met Herb Boyer in a California bar, and persuaded him to found a company, Genentech, in order to exploit the discovery. At the time, the barriers to success were very great. The FDA's regulations were even more stringent than they are today, and many scientists were strongly against any commercial exploitation of genetic manipulation until much more was known about the possible consequences.

Swanson, a classic entrepreneur, was undeterred. He managed to attract the scientists he needed to the company by his willingness to accept all kinds of flexible arrangements, unheard-of at the time, which allowed them to continue working at their universities, to get credit for academic papers that they wrote and sufficient money to purchase the equipment they needed. Swanson made deals with the major drug manufacturers to obtain the money for the research, which took years to complete.

In the 1970s Eli Lilly, a major pharmaceutical firm, was the market leader in the production of insulin for diabetics. Eli Lilly obtained the insulin from pigs, which had unsatisfactory side effects, and it knew that within two decades demand would exceed supply, so it held a competition for genetic reengineering researchers to see if it was possible to produce human insulin by transplanting human insulin genes into bacteria. Genentech and a number of universities entered the competition, which Genentech finally won, producing the first genetically engineered product, human insulin, in 1978. Because it was generated by bacteria, it could be produced in vast quantities at low cost.

The tiny firm was not in a strong negotiating position, and had to go to court before obtaining a $145 million settlement, a relatively small sum. However the success of the deal opened up the field, and the following year the firm engineered human growth hormone, used to treat dwarfism, which ultimately generated $2 billion in sales, establishing Genentech as a major player in the field.

HERE'S AN IDEA FOR YOU

In spite of all its faults, the US remains the best country to start an innovative business, largely because of the access to venture capital. Nowhere else will you find people willing and able to take a massive punt on a scheme just because they believe it's a good thing. The trick, though, is to have a genuinely groundbreaking and important innovation – and very few businesses have that.

49 NETWORKING

Women will swerve to avoid people they detest, or rush crying 'Darling!' towards people they detest even more.

In his chapter entitled 'Personality Screen', Parkinson describes how people behave at business-related parties, and parodies the scientific approach by describing how to measure the flow of people of varying status as they move around the room. He seems to have thought that doing such a thing would be ridiculous, but today a host of social scientists carry out exactly this kind of research. But is this research useful?

DEFINING IDEA

If a man does not make new acquaintance as he advances through life, he will soon find himself left alone. A man, Sir, should keep his friendship in constant repair.

SAMUEL JOHNSON, AUTHOR AND WIT

'Networking' is a big issue these days. Careers advisers tell you to network to get a job, and management gurus tell you to network to move up the career ladder. They are not wrong. It's only common sense to make contacts with people with whom you are trying to do business, and a chance meeting with someone at a conference might eventually lead to a profitable outcome in the future. However, adopting a scatter-gun approach and wildly networking with everyone you meet on the off-chance that one of them will work out is unlikely to be effective.

The work of the brilliant anthropologist Robin Dunbar sheds light on this issue. According to Dunbar, the closeness of relationships tends to form in layers, with a core group of about 5 people, a close group of 15, and outwards in layers that are limited at 50, 150, 500, and so on. The number of people in each relationship layer does vary, but not by much, and the findings are 'extremely robust', he says. 'Dunbar's number' – 150 – refers to the number of people you can have a relationship with where they are prepared to do you a favour.

Dunbar believes that the reasons for this limit are the amount of time available to invest in a relationship, and the cognitive difficulty in tracking the lives of more than 150 people. If you don't do both these things, he says, relationships will quickly decay and the individual will drop out of the 150 layer. The only exception to this is kinship relationships, which are lasting even when you don't see the person for many years.

This provides a useful insight into potential networking strategies. Are you networking because you are looking for people who can do you a favour? If so, according to this research, you will need to maintain the relationship, contacting them occasionally, and you probably won't be able to do this with more than 150 people. Or are you just seeking name recognition, where at some point in the future someone recognises who you are and, say, vouches for your identity at a business meeting? In that case, it's worth making contacts with perhaps 500 or 1000 people.

HERE'S AN IDEA FOR YOU

Dunbar's findings have interesting implications for networking sites like Facebook and LinkedIn. According to him, these internet sites won't help you to intensify relationships – which can only be done by personal contact – but they are useful in preventing people from dropping out of the 150 layer. He does not believe the sites really work for the layers further out.

50 PREDICTING THE FUTURE

In this, as in so many other matters, modern science is not at a loss.

In the early 1970s many experts were saying that oil would run out by 1980. In 2000 two prominent political commentators in the US, Robert Kagan and Bill Krystal, predicted that Iraq, Iran and North Korea would have nuclear missiles capable of reaching the United States by 2010. In 2008, a large survey of Wall Street analysts predicted that the stock market would continue to rise that year – in fact, it crashed.

DEFINING IDEA
One of the things I think we have learned is that we should all be very careful about making predictions about the future.
BILL CLINTON

Given that so many expert predictions fail, why do they continue to make them? The answer is, of course, that all individuals and organisations need to make plans for the future. The danger arises when people pretend to themselves or others that they can make consistently accurate forecasts. The performance of stock markets, for example, is notoriously hard to predict consistently, yet thousands of people in financial organisations make their livings by writing predictions that sound very confident.

Statistics provide planners with a wide range of sophisticated techniques that, when used appropriately, do rather better than 'naïve extrapolation', which means thinking that a phenomenon will follow the same pattern that it has in the past. Statisticians also provide useful estimates of how probable a particular outcome may be. Some things are easier to forecast than others, and most things are easier to forecast over the short term than the medium to long term. For instance, one study of large corporations found that sales forecasting errors doubled for periods in excess of two years in the future compared with forecasts for the month ahead, but were still only at 25%, which was considerably better than naïve extrapolation.

The difficulty of making long-term forecasts is one reason why many organisations focus on the short term. 'Short termism' is often criticised, but how useful is long-term forecasting likely to be? Back in the 1980s, when Japan was experiencing enormous economic success, Western countries were afraid that it was going to become the dominant economic power in the world. After a collapse in Japanese housing and stock markets in 1991, however, Japan went into the doldrums economically, and now attention has switched to China and India as the new rising economic superpowers. Many experts now forecast that China will surpass the US economically within ... well, they don't agree exactly when. And some of these forecasters seem simply to be extrapolating, based on China's current GDP growth, which we know is not a good way to make a forecast. Meanwhile, other experts are eagerly predicting that China's economy will collapse as Western countries become unable to buy its exports.

HERE'S AN IDEA FOR YOU

If you are faced with two conflicting professionally produced forecasts, should you just split the difference? 'No!', say the statisticians. If you are going to combine forecasts, you should use at least five forecasts that have employed substantially different methods or data. In cases where there is high uncertainty, you should give each forecast equal weight. The result, according to some researchers, will usually be as accurate as, or somewhat more accurate than, the typical component forecast.

51 INDIFFERENCE

There would seem to be a point beyond which the Chinese gains immunity from blackmail.

China's bureaucracy has very ancient roots (don't forget, 'mandarin' and 'kow-tow' are Chinese words), but that doesn't mean it has good control over all its officials. One of the main challenges facing the Chinese state is the sheer scale of the population. With the best will in the world, monitoring and directing the bureaucracy in a country of more than 1.3 billion people is a fantastically daunting task, and it is inevitable that many disasters occur due to bureaucratic misdeeds and indifference.

One of the biggest scandals of recent years was in the early 1990s, when many independent blood donation clinics were set up in the province of Henan. Donors, many of them poor peasants, were paid for their blood, which was sold on to hospitals. According to reports, local government officials appeared on television telling people to 'get rich' by selling blood. Henan's Health Bureau sold permits to set up the clinics, many of which were owned and operated by relatives of Health Bureau officials. Few precautions were taken; needles were reused, donors were not tested for diseases, and some donors used fake IDs to donate many times. Peasants began to camp outside the clinics so that they could donate several times a week. The worst practice was to collect blood plasma by putting the blood from several donors of the same

DEFINING IDEA

I prefer the folly of enthusiasm to the indifference of wisdom.

ANATOLE FRANCE, POET

blood type in a centrifuge and then reinjecting the mixed blood cells into the donors. Naturally, these unsafe practices led to an outbreak of HIV/AIDS and other diseases in the province.

By the late 1990s the provincial government in Henan was aware of the problem and began to close down the clinics. Simultaneously, it reacted fiercely to doctors and journalists who attempted to publicise the story, and did its best to present itself as heroically combating an epidemic of unknown origin. By 2001 the cat was out of the bag, and it was officially admitted that up to 50,000 people had been infected. In 2002 an HIV activist, Wan Yan Hai, was arrested in Beijing for publicising the scandal.

International health organisations have been reluctant to criticise China for fear that they would be prevented from participating in healthcare. One Chinese health professional I know studied HIV prevention in low-end prostitutes in rural China (who officially don't exist), and found that local authorities collude in many dangerous practices, such as the use of monthly intravenous antibiotic drips as a general prophylactic (which is useless against HIV/AIDS and promotes drug resistant mutations in other diseases). The problem, she says, is not a lack of scientific knowledge, or even a lack of resources: it's a bureaucratic indifference to people.

HERE'S AN IDEA FOR YOU

When you are planning to go abroad to an exotic location, here's an important point to consider. The rapid modernisation occurring in many countries has made it harder to assess personal risks, not only in health matters but also in questions such as whether to drive a car, or whether a certain area is dangerous. Make a list of potential risks, and do a proper risk assessment – don't just assume that everything works the way it does back home.

52 RETIREMENT

What are we ourselves to do when nearing the retirement age we have fixed for others? It will be obvious at once that our own case is entirely different from any other case we have so far considered ... It is with genuine reluctance that we agree to postpone our retirement for a few years, purely in the public interest.

In the final chapter of his book, Parkinson identifies the crux of the retirement issue: when we're young and moving up the career ladder, we are eager to get rid of the people at the top, but when we are at the top and approaching retirement age, we tend to want to go on working.

Most of the public discourse about retirement fails to make the distinction between having a great job and having a lousy one. If you are in a miserable, dead-end job, retirement – even early retirement – can look a lot more attractive than staying on. For instance, a friend of mine who taught television repair in a failing inner city school (where people were frequently stabbed in the corridors) was thrilled to be offered early retirement. But let's focus on the people who have desirable jobs and want to keep them.

Recently there has been a raft of older celebrities complaining about ageism. Madonna has complained that society doesn't allow older women to be sexy. Pierce Brosnan has blamed losing his James Bond role on ageism. The BBC has suffered a series of rows over the departure of older TV personalities, such as Arlene Philips, Anna Ford and Moira Stewart, and lost an employment tribunal case in 2011 against former *Countryfile* presenter Miriam O'Reilly, who was replaced on the show by a much younger presenter.

In UK universities there is a mandatory retirement age, and older boffins are becoming more vocal in their complaints about the system. Peter Lawrence, a zoologist, argues that successful older scientists bring in much more money to their universities (by attracting research grants) than they cost, and says that the American system, which bans mandatory retirement for most jobs, is more meritocratic.

Improvements in life expectancy and health have created generations of fit, able older people who want to go on working. Currently, life expectancy at 65 is 85 for women and 82.4 for men, and is expected to go on rising. We can therefore expect a lot more anti-ageist activism in the future. But let's not forget what the issue is really about: a vicious competition for desirable jobs in a world where there aren't enough jobs to go around. Will age and experience beat youth and vigour? We'll have to wait and see.

HERE'S AN IDEA FOR YOU

Politicians have seized upon freelancing for older people as a way to solve the retirement problem, and on the surface it may look attractive, offering the chance of more freedom, working from home, and picking the jobs that suit you. But if you have never done it before, be careful. A recent study of the media industry by Dr Kerry Platman found that, although some older freelancers enjoyed a lucrative career, the majority did not, suffering from low pay and extreme insecurity. So don't assume that going freelance is all roses, and go in with your eyes open.

INDEX

G

H

I

J

K

L

M